Museums of London

Westholme Museum Guides

Museums of London

A Guide for Residents and Visitors

Paul Skinner

WITHDRAWN

WESTHOLME
Yardley

Acknowledgments
To Laura Waldron and Bruce Franklin, who suggested it; to numerous museum personnel who, either knowingly or otherwise, assisted; and to those who have suggested, reminded and puzzled over why I seemed to have no other topic of conversation: Andrew Gilman, Philip Young, Max Saunders. Above all, as ever, to Naomi.

Published by Westholme Publishing, LLC, Eight Harvey Avenue, Yardley, Pennsylvania 19067.

10 9 8 7 6 5 4 3 2 1
First Printing

ISBN: 978-1-59416-048-6

ISBN 10: 1-59416-048-1

Visit our Web site: www.westholmepublishing.com

Printed in the United States of America on acid-free paper.

For my mother

MARIE SKINNER

Contents

Introduction

One of the world's great cities, London had several beginnings, or at least tells different versions of its beginning. Some say that a wandering Trojan prince, Brutus, part of the great diaspora after the sacking of Troy by the Greek armies, voyaged west under the guidance of the goddess Diana, sailed up a great river, and defeated the race of giants led by Gog and Magog (or, perhaps, slew Gog at a great battle in Totnes) before founding the city of New Troy, which was then, a millennium later, rebuilt and renamed by King Lud, first as Caerlud ("city of Lud" in Welsh), later in a corrupted form as "Caerlundein." Less contested are the city's Roman beginnings, rooted in tireless archaeological investigation and more orthodox research. In the Museum of London, the city's chronology really begins, as all such stories must, with that great river, the Thames. With the technology available to them in the first century, the Romans forded it at the first practical point as they advanced northwest from their landing-place in present-day Kent. Their settlement of Londinium, on the river's north bank, soon became the primary city in the province of Britannia. Then followed its eventual abandonment to the Saxons in the early fifth century, as the great empire staggered under the shock of Rome's sacking by the forces of

Alaric the Visigoth, and the legions withdrew. In the ninth century, Danish forces occupied London, but Alfred the Great recaptured it, transforming and strengthening the city. When Edward the Confessor had a Benedictine church rebuilt as Westminster Abbey, both palace and place of government, London was confirmed as the political centre of the kingdom. William the Conqueror was crowned in the Abbey on Christmas Day, 1066. The city continued to grow, and trade to flourish, throughout the medieval period, surviving the Black Death, which killed a third of the population, as it later withstood the Great Plague — and the Great Fire of London that followed it.

At the time of the Norman invasion in 1066, London was by far the largest city in England. By 1700, its population had reached half a million, which doubled by the great 1801 census; a century more and it was, by some margin, the world's largest city: its population more than half as much again as New York City's and well over twice that of Paris. Prime Minister and novelist Benjamin Disraeli had written of London as a nation rather than a city and, at the time of this writing, it is exactly 100 years since Ford Madox Ford's *The Soul of London* asserted that "England is a small island, the world is infinitesimal among the planets. But London is illimitable." He was referring to a city of the mind and memory, the city as a collection of impressions — cumulative and overlaid — as much as one of houses, shops, and churches. Still, the London of bricks and mortar remains the largest city in Western Europe, and the most cosmopolitan, with over 300 languages spoken across the huge expanse of Greater London. When Ford wrote, a quarter of a century and a World War later, "This then was the last of England, the last of London . . . ," part of what saddened and enraged him was the development of political policies that would fiercely limit immigration to the country's shores. A topical theme, indeed. Ford understood that England had been made by immigrants—by Huguenots and Anabaptists, Flemish weavers and Jewish merchants—and that England's great strength and value to the world lay precisely in having evolved ways in which people of disparate backgrounds and cultural traditions might live and work together in mutual tolerance and respect. And, of course, the numberless stories of immigrant communities and histories, voyages, scatterings, survivals and disappearances are inextricably entwined with almost every museum and major collection that follows.

London has been the capital city and focal point of one of the greatest empires in history, which has meant, predominantly, trade, finance, military, and naval forces and revolutions on the largest national and international scale in production, distribution, and marketing. But it has also been the magnet that has drawn individual men and women (and, too often, mere boys and girls) not only from the distant towns and villages or obscure country parishes in Cornwall and Yorkshire and Scotland, it has drawn them across seas, across continents, across the whole world. And it has done so not only in the prosaic ways of offering the means of economic advancement but very often with some measure of enchantment, with more than a breath of fairytale; not merely wealth but unimaginable riches; not merely fame but fantastic celebrity.

It has often been remarked that London is accidental, haphazard, without logic or overall design, a collection of villages or distinct localities tumbled and jumbled together. Historians note that there has never been a tyrant with both the power and the desire to raze it and start again, to remake the capital in his or her own image. The only great destroyers in the modern period have been the Great Fire of London in 1666 and the Luftwaffe during the Blitz: the aftermaths of both produced radical rebuilding and remaking of the capital.

In the early nineteenth century, William Cobbett called it "the Great Wen," hating its irresistible sucking in of people, power, and money; impoverishing the countryside; and ruining the lives of many who made their way there, lured by its gaudy and seductive promises. And, indeed, London still exerts a powerful and, to many people, wholly disproportionate force, skewing the distribution of influence, wealth, and concern. The many vibrant and distinctive regions of Britain—distinctive in their landscape, their arts, their cultural traditions, their economic success—sometimes manifest a deep unease about the constant focus on London from foreign visitors, businesses, official bodies, cultural commentators, and artists in every medium. And, of course, the city is vast, exhausting (to contemplate, let alone navigate), labyrinthine, and often baffling. But, for all that, London remains, as it has long been, wholly irresistible. Visitors in their tens of millions—half of them from overseas—come for its shops, theatres, restaurants, palaces, pubs, churches, great houses, art galleries, and, of course, museums. Or they come simply to walk its streets and stroll through its parks and public gardens and along its riverside paths.

The literature of, and about, London is on a comparable scale to the city itself. Almost every major writer has written of it, and many have lived in it for a greater or shorter period, while some are often closely and specifically identified with it: from Shakespeare, Marlowe, Ben Jonson, Pepys, Dickens, Samuel

Johnson, William Blake, and Virginia Woolf through to such contemporary writers as Peter Ackroyd and Iain Sinclair. Henry Mayhew and Charles Booth documented its poor in devastating detail. Monet came to paint it, as did Canaletto; Handel came, and Wagner, and Karl Marx. From the United States came Benjamin Franklin and John Adams, Emerson and Whistler, Hawthorne and Henry James, Ezra Pound, and T. S. Eliot. Architectural historians, local historians, lawyers, bankers, cartographers, walkers, ghost hunters, and geographers have written literally thousands of reference books, guides, histories, pamphlets, polemics, and poems about the city — loving it, loathing it, longing for it, murmuring or shouting in the midst of it, trawling memories sixty minutes or sixty years old: memoirs of childhood, war, crime, love, and loss. They are being written now, of course, and will be published in two months or twenty years or never, commemorating or marking recent events, incidents of wonder or dreadfulness, apparently dramatic changes; but, one suspects, the long history of London will not be much changed. Or rather, since the one constant in this city's story, as in the stories of other great cities, no doubt, is change — ceaseless, tireless, relentless change (though not at a constant pace) — that will remain the case.

Many communities in London — and of course the country as a whole — have intimate and not always comfortable relationships with Britain's imperial history. So much of the country's wealth came from the West Indies, so much of its story is bound up with the Indian sub-continent or "the scramble for Africa": this means war, slavery, and conquest as well as spices, sugar, and rum. London's museums tell endless stories of Britain's imperial past, often without such explicit intention, yet they can hardly do otherwise than tell such tales, of expropriation, of souvenir hunting, of dreams of unbounded wealth, imperial assumption — or, sometimes, such fierce admiration for an artefact, a picture, a piece of carved stone that its possession must be achieved at any price. There are narratives of social history, economic history, the professionalization of groups, the evolution of workshops, guilds, brotherhoods, and unions. There are also frequent recurrences of another narrative: the individual collection, one man's (almost always a man's) immense range of interests and indefatigable desire to collect and satisfy curiosity combined with the necessary fortune and, sometimes, the equally necessary obsessive nature. It might be a few dozen or a few hundred pieces of art, a thousand or even tens of thousands of objects, stone fragments, bone fragments, jewels and masks, axe heads and shrunken heads, which hugely augment the holdings of a museum or gallery and which even, sometimes, furnish the solid basis for, say, a great, even a world-class museum. There are royal collections and palaces aplenty, but it is not in such settings that a great deal of the history of Britain's museums is actually told.

There are single, though complex, narrative threads, such as that concerned with the history of medicine and its related disciplines, which can be traced all over London through surgeons, apothecaries, dentists, ophthalmologists, anaesthetists, psychiatrists, and the like. Another runs through some of the many gardens worthy of notice, beautifully suggested in the Museum of Garden History, with its resonant ghosts of the John Tradescants, linking plant hunters and explorers, traders and collectors, and the gardens themselves, walled or moated, herb gardens and knot gardens, ranging from the healing acres of the Chelsea Physic Garden to the spot in the garden of Thomas Carlyle's house where the philosopher's dog lies buried. Elements of other stories lie easily at hand, such as the Bramah Museum's history of tea and coffee juxtaposed with the Cutty Sark clipper ship, a survivor of that trade, one of the great ships that raced the tea across the world, and with the Museum in Docklands, its warehouse home an eminent survivor of the huge and astonishingly varied trade centred on those docks. Many museums hoard evidence and stories of a military or naval past, of exploration, above all of commerce in every corner of the known—and constantly expanding—world. And there are many houses of tremendous historic interest and importance, some of them grand mansions of aristocratic pretensions and grandeur but more often houses commissioned by mightily successful merchants, lavishly equipped with artefacts, paintings, and antiquities from all over the world. The continuing archaeological research into the history and origins of London reveals more and more the layers, quite literally, of historical periods, unsurprisingly, no doubt, in a city of such temporal and physical depths.

The history of Britain's museums and galleries is in part, of course, a history of political juggling. Through the long nineteenth century, crowded with revolutions and historical upheavals, the liberal-minded middle class and those patricians concerned with the state of the nation gradually extended the cultural and political and, eventually, electoral landscapes that the poorer classes might inhabit. A question, sometimes implicit, behind the opening of, or increase in access to, several major institutions was: would exposure to such cultural riches humanize rather than inflame? Would it produce a more civilized, more cultivated populace rather than fanning the embers of their revolutionary zeal? We don't ask such questions now or, rather, we phrase them very differently, but whatever the phrasing, having seen the extraordinary troops of schoolchildren in the Great Court of the British Museum, or the man and the woman sitting together, rapt, motionless, gazing at a painting in the National Gallery, and having watched the child in the Museum of London stop stock still in front of the Roman village and hug herself with glee, my answer is strongly affirmative.

Finally — if "London" is so huge, where do you stop? Where, that is to say, does this guide stop? There are museums, great houses, celebrated places of immense interest in what are, technically, the counties of Surrey or Middlesex or Kent, which have been relegated to a brief appendix of such destinations: Further Afield. Recalling the old story of two judges taking leave of one another ("Remember, if you can't be just, be arbitrary!"), I've employed the postcode as final court of appeal, limiting the main entries to those museums having addresses that employ the London postcodes.

On the matter of exclusions, I should add that I've attempted to banish the personal from the following entries. Perceptions of a place vary hugely, and the main point of this guide is information rather than opinion. My admiration and, often, strong affection for the British Museum, for the National Gallery, for the Freud Museum, for Sir John Soane's Museum, for Tate Britain, for the V & A — and quite a few others — are, I suspect, quite easily detectable. I've not set out to conceal or mislead. But I've tried to nudge my likes and dislikes to the periphery, to leave a clearer, less cluttered space in which the reader — and the museum visitor — can inscribe his or her own.

Using *Museums of London*

For the purposes of this book, a museum is defined as a "permanent collection," open to the public, of predominantly non-reproduction artefacts. A significant number of institutions have consequently been excluded because they are solely temporary exhibition spaces; a few are, due to specific circumstances (usually lack of space) currently unable to offer ready access to their permanent collections, a notable example being the Ben Uri Gallery (the London Jewish Museum of Art), reluctantly removed for that reason. Of course, a considerable number of those included have frequent and, in many cases, internationally significant temporary exhibitions alongside their permanent collections. There are also several institutions which, though often very well-known indeed, seem to me to be primarily tourist destinations rather than museum collections: Madame Tussaud's and the London Dungeon are examples of this category. Finally, I've omitted a few buildings, of undoubted interest to industrial archaeologists, that I couldn't really classify as museums.

The museums in this guide are listed in alphabetical order by the primary name of the museum or collection. Each entry provides the address, phone number and Web site for the museum as well as the hours of operation and admission prices and policies. Detailed directions are not given but every visitor to the city should obtain a copy of the indispensable *London A-Z* which also lists many museums (and other major visitor attractions) in its index .

Two things, at least, stand out immediately when surveying the museums and galleries of London: firstly, the sheer number

and variety, and the number of institutions which are of international or world importance; secondly, the proportion, almost
exactly one-half, which charge no admission fee. There are several major museums that, while maintaining a policy of free
admission to the permanent collections, sometimes charge for
entry to some temporary exhibitions. There are also many
museums that offer free admission, as a matter of principle,
but, nevertheless, rely on voluntary contributions to maintain
their collections and access to them, so contributions are always
welcome and often vital. Admission prices given here should,
of course, be treated warily. In a few cases, up-to-date information could not be confirmed and the entry will consist of
the phrase "admission charge." The term "concessions" carries
a number of varying connotations but senior citizens, those in
receipt of unemployment benefit and full-time students will
qualify most frequently. The cut-off points by age for the
under-16s vary enormously and comprise an absorbing study in
themselves.

Outside of the largest museums, and particularly if you are
making a special or extended trip out of the centre, it is always
advisable to phone ahead to check. Circumstances change,
often with little warning. Small museums are sometimes staffed
by volunteers and are particularly vulnerable to sudden local
crises.

Public Holidays are an intriguing and sometimes playful area
of British cultural life and there are no wholly reliable rules for
what opens and what closes on such days — or, sometimes,
when they occur — but there are guidelines. At Easter, Good
Friday and the following Monday are public holidays. In May,
the first and last Mondays are public holidays, as is the last

Monday in August. Christmas Day, Boxing Day and New Year's Day are also, reliably, public holidays. Some business-es—and museums and galleries—close over the Christmas period, from Christmas Eve through to the 2nd of January. There are no solid rules here, however, and checking is always advisable if there is any room for doubt.

Further Reading and Resources

There are, quite literally, thousands of books about London, ranging from immensely scholarly works on architecture, Victorian engineering and the history of public parks to popu-lar compilations about famous murderers, urban legends and fashions of the 1920s. Any selection from such a huge range is likely to seem arbitrary but here is a brief list of enjoyable and informative titles which are currently available.

Peter Ackroyd, *London: The Biography* (Vintage in the UK; Anchor in the US). Long, immensely readable, anecdotal, with an invaluable bibliography, 'An Essay on Sources,' which can be roamed through a little like London itself.

Ford Madox Ford's *The Soul of London* is available now in *England and the English*, edited by Sara Haslam (Carcanet).

Samuel Pepys' famous *Diary* is published in many editions, currently in ten volumes (plus an index) or, more manageably, in paperback selections from Penguin in the UK and Random House in the US. Claire Tomalin's illuminating biography, *Samuel Pepys: The Unequalled Self*, is published by Penguin in the UK and Vintage in the US.

Liza Picard's *Elizabeth's London*, *Restoration London*, *Dr Johnson's London*, and *Victorian London*, published by Phoenix in the UK and St Martin's Griffin in the US, are very readable and densely detailed accounts of everyday life in the London of the sixteenth, seventeenth, eighteenth and nineteenth centuries.

V. S. Pritchett, *London Observed*. Available from Penguin in the UK and David R. Godine in the US. First published nearly half a century ago but superbly written and, with photographs by Evelyn Hofer, wonderfully evocative.

The great artist William Hogarth is one of the central figures in London's story and Jenny Uglow's biography, *Hogarth* (Faber in the UK; Farrar, Straus and Giroux in the US) is, among much else, a wonderful recreation of eighteenth-century London in all its grime and glamour.

The novelist A. N. Wilson assembled *The Faber Book of London*, a marvellously wide-ranging anthology which honours both the familiar and the obscure.

Quite apart from the innumerable histories and guides, there is a dizzying choice of novels, stories, poems and plays, essays, biographies and memoirs which illuminate every period of London's history: a random gathering might include Charles Dickens, Arthur Conan Doyle, Patrick Hamilton, H.G. Wells, Ben Jonson, John Dryden, James Boswell, Virginia Woolf, Julian Maclaren Ross, Elizabeth Bowen and Iain Sinclair.

Visitor Information

Britain and London Visitor Centre

1 Regent Street, Piccadilly, London SW1Y 4XT

Open: M, 9:30 AM–6:30 PM; Tu–F, 9:00 AM–6:30 PM; Sa–Su, 10:00 AM–4:00 PM

Underground: Piccadilly

London Information Centre

Leicester Square, London W1

020 7292 2333

www.londoninformation.org

Visit London

020 7932 2000

www.visitlondon.com

Transportation

The vast majority of the museums in this book are reachable by tube and the nearest underground station is included in each entry. Many museums are, in fact, in walking distance of one another, often occurring in clusters or groups (as indicated on the map) which may reassure and, perhaps, stimulate the determined museumgoer. Some of the museums listed in the "Further Afield" appendix require travel by the conventional railway system and occasionally a bus journey: the relevant entry normally indicates this.

Map

Most of the museums in this book are within the radius of the Underground lines around central London. Each number on the following map refers to a museum's page in the book. The map is designed to show the reader the general proximity of the museums to one another and not their exact locations.

Museums of London

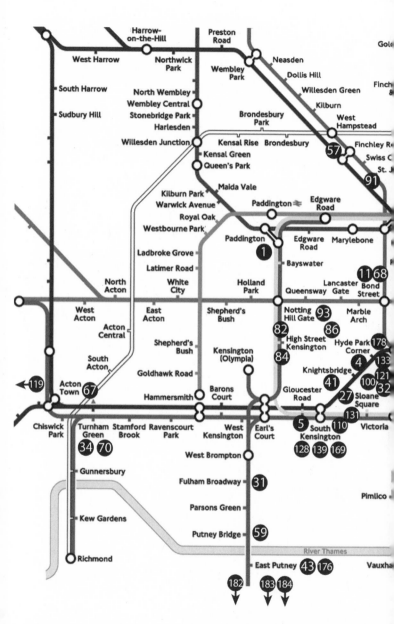

Each number is the museum's page in the book.

Visual Codes

Architecturally significant

Exhibits suitable for children

Food available on premises

Notable art

Notable grounds or garden

Science oriented

Site of historic event

Alexander Fleming Laboratory Museum

St. Mary's Hospital, Praed Street, Paddington, London W2 1NY
020 7886 6528
www.st-marys.nhs.uk/fleming_museum.html

Open: M–Th, 10:00 AM–1:00 PM; other times by appointment only;
closed on public holidays and between Christmas and New Year
Admission: £2.00; Concessions, £1.00
No disabled access to the museum; many stairs. Groups welcome: to
arrange your visit, please contact the curator.
Underground: Paddington
Buses: 7, 15, 27, 36

This small laboratory is the one in which the Scottish bacteriologist, Alexander Fleming, was working when he discovered penicillin in September 1928. It is now carefully restored to its condition at that time, and visitors are taken back to a period in which there were no antibiotics to fight often life-threatening bacteria. While working on the influenza virus, Fleming returned from holiday to find that a mould that had developed in a Petri dish had created a bacteria-free area around itself. He christened the active element penicillin. It was ten years before Fleming's discovery was thoroughly developed by a group at Oxford, but it revolutionized medicine, and penicillin remains one of the most important antibiotics. Fleming was awarded the Nobel Prize in 1945, and the story of his work is vividly told here by means of displays and videos.

All Hallows Undercroft Museum

Byward Street, London EC3 5BJ
020 7481 2928
www.allhallowsbythetower.org.uk

Open: M–F, 11:00 AM–4:00 PM; Sa–Su, 11:00 AM–5:00 PM (church is open longer hours)
Admission: Free
Underground: Tower Hill

All Hallows is the church from which Samuel Pepys watched the destructive progress of the Great Fire of London in 1666. In his diary, he praised the efforts of workmen from the King's yards, sent by Pepys's friend, Sir William Penn, father of the founder of Pennsylvania, who was baptized here in 1644. All Hallows, "the oldest church in the City of London," was also the setting for John Quincy Adams' wedding to Louisa Johnson in 1797, and the relevant marriage register is displayed here, beneath a portrait of Adams. Seriously damaged during the Second World War, the church was reconstructed under the direction of Lord Mottistone, who also excavated beneath the building. There are fragments of three Saxon crosses and, among other Saxon and Roman remains, ashes from Boudicca's burning of London in AD 60 and part of a second-century Roman tessellated pavement. Below the present high altar, the chapel contains altar stones brought back to All Hallows from Castle Athlit, south of Haifa in present-day Israel, originally built by the Crusaders and with strong links to the Knights Templar.

Anaesthesia Museum

Anaesthesia Heritage Centre, Association of Anaesthetists of Great
Britain and Ireland, 21 Portland Place, London W1B 1PY
020 7631 1650
www.aagbi.org/heritage/museum.htm

Open: M–F, 9:00 AM–5:00 PM
Appointment recommended; bookings for groups of up to fifteen people can be made on request. Talks and guided tours are also available.
Admission: Free
Underground: Oxford Circus/Regents Park/Great Portland Street

Begun in 1953 with the donation by A. Charles King of his
extensive collection of historical apparatus, the museum covers
the history of anaesthesia from the late eighteenth century
through to highly sophisticated contemporary appliances. The
landmark case for general medical practice was William
Morton's use of ether at the Massachusetts General Hospital
in Boston in October 1846 (the museum's exhibits include a
replica of his ether inhalation demonstrator) and, two months
later, a dental surgeon, James Robinson, administered the first
ether anaesthetic in England. The museum's space is limited,
which means that, in practice, only a proportion of the association's nearly 3,000 artefacts can be shown at any one time,
though most of the material can be viewed if notice is given.
The larger anaesthetic machines are kept elsewhere, though
they are sometimes incorporated into travelling and temporary
exhibitions, and detailed information about them is available
here.

Apsley House Wellington Museum

Hyde Park Corner, 149 Piccadilly, London W1J 7NT
020 7499 5676
www.english-heritage.org.uk

Open: T–Su, 10:00 AM–5:00 PM, 1 Apr–31 Oct (and Bank Holiday
Mondays); T–Su, 10:00 AM–4:00 PM, 1 Nov–31 Mar; closed 24–26
Dec and 1 Jan.
Admission: £5.30; Concessions, £4.00; Children, £2.70. Joint ticket
with Wellington Arch: £6.90; Concessions, £5.20; Children, £3.50
Underground: Hyde Park Corner

Arthur Wellesley, first Duke of Wellington, made Apsley
House his London home after a dazzling military career, cul-
minating in his victory over Napoleon at Waterloo in 1815.
Wellington enlarged the house (originally designed and built by
Robert Adam, 1771–1778), adding the magnificent Waterloo
Gallery by Benjamin Dean Wyatt. The seventh Duke gave the
house and contents to the nation in 1947, and after renovation
and repair to the damage inflicted during the Second World
War, it was opened to the public as a museum in 1952. The
gallery holds a collection particularly strong in Spanish and
British narrative art and features work by Rubens, Goya,
Velasquez, and Brueghel as well as porcelain, silver, sculpture,
furniture, medals, and memorabilia. A gigantic statue of
Napoleon by Canova dominates the hall. The house was popularly referred to as "No. 1, London" because it was the first
that the traveller encountered after passing the tollgates in
Knightsbridge. The family continues to occupy a suite of private rooms here.

Baden-Powell House

65-67 Queen's Gate, London SW7 5JS
020 7584 7031
www.scoutbase.org.uk

🍽

Open: Daily
Admission: Free
Underground: South Kensington/Gloucester Road

Baden-Powell House functions both as a budget hostel and as a conference centre. It is also a focus for the international Scouting and Guiding community and houses a small permanent exhibition telling the life story of Robert Baden-Powell (1857–1941), military man and defender of Mafeking in the Boer War. In 1908, he founded the Boy Scout movement and, with his sister Agnes, began the Girl Guide movement two years later. The Scout Association now operates in more than a hundred countries.

The exhibition describes the birth and growth of scouting from its origins on Brownsea Island in Dorset to its establishment as a worldwide movement by the time of Baden-Powell's death. There is a video wall with a continuous film showing highlights of Baden-Powell's life. The first of two other related sites is the campsite, located in Gilwell Park, Bury Road, Chingford, London (Tel: 020 8498 5410), which was given to the Scout Movement in 1919. It includes several displays and the caravan Baden-Powell was given at a famous jamboree in 1929. Secondly, the mill house on Wimbledon Common, in which Baden-Powell once lived, is now the site of the Wimbledon Windmill Museum (see separate entry below).

Bank of England Museum

Bartholomew Lane, Threadneedle Street, London EC2R 8AH

020 7601 5545

www.bankofengland.co.uk/education/museum

Open: M–F, 10:00 AM–5:00 PM; Christmas Eve, 10:00 AM–1:00 PM; closed public holidays.

Admission: Free

Underground: Bank

The Bank of England dates from 1694, when it was set up to facilitate the funding of foreign wars. Sir John Soane, whose own museum is at Lincoln's Inn Fields, was responsible for designing the 1788 building on the present site, though no more than the exterior wall survives of his original, the rest having been destroyed during the bank's enlargement in the 1920s and 1930s. There is a reconstruction of Soane's stock office as it was in 1793. Several displays illustrate the changes in appearance of British currency, together with printing and engraving equipment, weights, and measures. There are examples of every type of coin and banknote, including an extensive collection of forgeries, as well as documents bearing the signatures of George Washington, Lord Nelson, and others. In addition to prints, cartoons, caricatures, and paintings, there are two busts by Joseph Nollekens of famous political rivals William Pitt the Younger and Charles James Fox and a statue of William III by Henry Cheere, commissioned by the bank in 1732. Visitors can also see some of the muskets and pikes that were kept to defend the bank, and paperweights made from used banknotes are on sale in the museum's gift shop.

Banqueting House

Whitehall Palace, Whitehall, London SW1A 2ER

020 3166 6150; information line (recorded outside office hours): 0870 751 5178

www.hrp.org.uk

Open: M–Sa, 10:00 AM–5:00 PM. Sometimes closed for official functions—please telephone to check; closed Sundays, Bank Holidays, and 24 Dec–1 Jan (inclusive).

Admission: Adults, £4.50; Students (with ID) and senior citizens, £3.50; Children under 16, £2.25; Children under 5, Free

Underground: Westminster/Embankment/Charing Cross

Designed for James I by Inigo Jones, this impressive building, completed in 1622, is all that remains of Whitehall Palace, the sovereign's principal residence from 1530 until 1698, when it was destroyed by fire. The Banqueting House was originally used not only for state occasions but also for the frequent performance of plays and masques. The remarkable ceiling paintings by Peter Paul Rubens were produced in his Antwerp workshop, shipped to England in October 1635, and installed the following year. They were commissioned by Charles I to celebrate the life and government of his father, James I. Perhaps the building is most famous for being the scene of Charles's execution in 1649, on a scaffold erected against its walls. Ironically, it was also where Charles II was enthusiastically received by both houses of Parliament on his restoration to the throne in 1660. After the disastrous 1698 fire, the building was used as a chapel until 1890, and then became the museum of the Royal United Services Institute. Restored internally to its early seventeenth-century appearance, the Banqueting House is still used for state functions.

Benjamin Franklin House

36 Craven Street, London WC2N 5NF

020 7930 9121

www.thersa.org/franklin

Open: W–Su, Noon–5:00 PM

Tickets are collected from the nearby New Players Theatre (Villiers Street, The Arches). Visitors should arrive at the theatre at least 10 minutes prior to the beginning of each showing: these are at noon, 1:00 PM, 2:00 PM, 3:15 PM and 4:15 PM.

Admission: Adults £5.00, Children under 16, Free

Underground: Charing Cross

Benjamin Franklin (1706–1790), scientist, diplomat, philosopher, printer, author, inventor and Founding Father of the United States, made his first visit to England in late 1724, remaining some eighteen months. This is the house in which he subsequently lived for nearly sixteen years between 1757 and 1775, an elegant Georgian building notable for its simplicity and clarity of design. In the thirty years between Franklin's trips to England, he had become an extraordinarily influential figure, founding the postal and fire services, the Pennsylvania Hospital and the academy that became the University of Pennsylvania. The Royal Society of London had already awarded him the Copley Medal in recognition of his advances in the theory of electricity, and later unanimously elected him a member of the Society. While lodging at 36 Craven Street, Franklin pursued his many scientific and cultural interests and maintained his existing contacts with leading figures. He worked on his energy-saving stove and the bifocal spectacles that he later perfected in Paris; invented the glass harmonica for which Bach,

Beethoven and Mozart subsequently composed; wrote many letters and articles; and was also, necessarily, engaged in delicate political negotiations, on the eve of the American Revolution, in his official capacity of colonial agent of the Pennsylvania Assembly.

Benjamin Franklin House, built circa 1730, opened to the public in January 2006, to mark the tercentenary of his birth, after an extensive programme of restoration. While school visitors and researchers will probably gravitate to the Student Science Centre and the Scholarship Centre, most visitors to the house will engage in the "Historical Experience," a live dramatic performance which moves through a succession of uncluttered and attractive rooms, integrated with the extensive use of audiovisual material which vividly presents the historical context in which both private and public events in Franklin's life occurred, using many of his own words to present a striking and arresting portrait of the man and his times. Beginning with a brief introductory film in the basement, where some of the artefacts from the conservation programme are on display, visitors ascend in the company of Polly Hewson, daughter of Franklin's landlady, who became his "second daughter." Illustrations of the dramatic and hazardous nature of the period are intercut by revealing, often amusing and sometimes poignant details of Franklin's domestic routines and predilections, and his efforts to maintain close contacts with his wife and friends during the long period of separation. As the sole surviving Franklin home and, in effect, the first United States Embassy, the house has an unsurprisingly special status in Anglo-American history.

Bramah Museum of Tea and Coffee

40 Southwark Street, London SE1 1UN
020 7403 5650
www.bramahmuseum.co.uk

Open: Daily, 10:00 AM–6:00 PM; closed Christmas Day and Boxing
Day.
Admission: £4.00; Concessions, £3.50
Underground: London Bridge

The Bramah Museum presents the history of tea and coffee
since their arrival in Europe from the Far East and Africa
through its ceramics, metalware, prints, and other displays.
Britain played a major role in both the China tea trade and the
development of production in India, Ceylon, and Africa,
though it was Dutch merchants that initiated the commercial
importing of tea into Europe early in the seventeenth century.
The London tea trade has traditionally conducted its blending
and packing activities close to London Bridge, and the East
India Company's sailing ships would unload their cargoes from
China on the Thames. Numerous episodes in the narrative of
Britain's tea heritage are explained and illustrated here with the
aid of maps, diagrams, and engravings. There is also an extensive display of coffee machines, café sets, and equipment of all
kinds and practical explanations of the history of coffee from
its origins in the Middle East and India through its seventeenth-century emergence in the capitals of Europe to the
explosion of coffee-bar culture from the 1950s onwards.
Visitors can sample the museum's wares in the reassuringly
authentic tea room.

British Dental Association Museum

64 Wimpole Street, London W1G 8YS

0207 935 0875

www.bda.org/museum

Open: Tu and Th, 1:00 PM–4:00 PM; other times by appointment.
During holidays please telephone before visiting.

Admission: Free

Underground: Bond Street

In 1919, the association's librarian, Lilian Lindsay, who had become the first qualified woman dentist in 1892, donated several old dental instruments that had been stored in a box under her bed. From this humble beginning, the BDA Museum, which opened its doors to the general public in 1967, now houses an internationally significant collection of over 20,000 objects. The holdings illustrate the whole story of dentistry in the United Kingdom, from brutal medieval practices through the crucial introduction of anaesthesia to more recent developments in professional dentistry. The collections include instruments and equipment, furniture, archives, photographs, and paintings. Among the notable items are ivory dentures made with real teeth retrieved from the bodies of soldiers killed at the Battle of Waterloo and toothbrushes carved out of bone. Visitors can also view early health campaign footage put together by George Cunningham, the father of preventive dentistry.

British Library

96 Euston Road, King's Cross, London NW1 2DB
020 7412 7332
www.bl.uk

Open: M and W–F, 9:30 AM–6:00 PM; Tu, 9:30 AM–8:00 PM; Sa,
9:30 AM–5:00 PM; Su and Public Holidays, 11:00 AM–5:00 PM
Admission: Free
Underground: King's Cross

When an act of Parliament brought about the opening of the
British Library in 1973, it incorporated several existing institutions, including the library departments of the British
Museum. The British Museum's Department of Printed
Books had been founded in 1753, when the museum itself
began, and had grown into one of the world's largest libraries.
The British Library now houses the national collection of
books, manuscripts, and maps, based on three seminal individual collections: those of Sir John Sloane, Sir Robert Cotton,
and Robert Harley, First Earl of Oxford. In a remarkable glass
tower, running through six floors, are the 60,000 volumes
donated by George III in 1823 from his collection.

The British Library, in its privileged function of legal deposito-
ry, receives a copy of every publication produced in the United
Kingdom and Ireland, and three million new items are incorporated into its holdings each year. These holdings are so rich
that it is difficult even to hint at the extent and variety of them.
But they include the earliest dated printed book, the *Diamond
Sutra*, which can be seen in the exhibition galleries alongside
many other national treasures. There is a copy of Gutenberg's

forty-two–line Bible, from about 1455, the earliest book to be printed in Europe using movable type; Captain Scott's diary from the tragic 1911–1912 expedition to the South Pole; and a copy of the first edition of what is probably the most famous newspaper in the world, *The Times*, issued on 18 March 1788. The library holds two of the four surviving copies of *Magna Carta* (the others are at Lincoln and Salisbury), the fundamental document in the history of British rights and liberties. There is the original manuscript of *Alice's Adventures in Wonderland* (1862–1862), which Lewis Carroll wrote for Alice Liddell, and a copy of the First Folio of Shakespeare's plays. An English copy of the "Plan of New York" produced for the Dutch authorities by Jacques Courtelyou is dated 1664; and other treasures range from a manuscript of the ancient Sanskrit epic, *Ramayana*, through the Arundel Codex (manuscript sheets of Leonardo da Vinci's notes and diagrams) and a recording of Nelson Mandela's trial speech to the Latin manuscript of *The Lindisfarne Gospels*, probably made on Holy Island in Northumbria around the close of the seventh century. The manuscript contains the earliest translation of the Gospels into English, added between the lines in the late tenth century.

In more general terms, the library's holdings include material from 300 BC to today's newspapers. There are in excess of 310,000 manuscript volumes, from Jane Austen to James Joyce to Handel; 49.5 million patents; over four million maps; and at least 260,000 journal titles. In all, the collection includes 150 million items in most known languages. The Sound Archive keeps sound recordings from nineteenth-century cylinders to the latest CD, DVD, and minidisc recordings, and the library houses eight million stamps and other philatelic items.

Apparently, seeing just five items a day would necessitate spending some 80,000 years to see the whole of the collection, an impressive life span. The British Library has on-site space for over 1,200 readers, and over 16,000 people use the collections each day. The library also operates the world's largest document delivery service, providing millions of items a year to customers all over the world.

British Museum

Great Russell Street, London WC1B 3DG
020 7323 8000
www.thebritishmuseum.ac.uk

Open: 10:00 AM–5:30 PM (selected galleries until 8:30 PM, Th and F); closed 24–26 Dec, 1 Jan, and Good Friday.

Admission: Free

Underground: Tottenham Court Road/Holborn/Russell Square

The oldest public museum in the world—and one of the very greatest—was founded in 1753 and opened to the public on 15 January 1759. With the exception of two World Wars, when parts of the collection were evacuated, it has remained open ever since, gradually increasing both its opening hours and its attendance from perhaps 5,000 a year to today's five million. The initial impetus for the new museum came from the physician, naturalist, and collector, Sir Hans Sloane (1660–1753), president of the Royal College of Physicians and of the Royal Society, who left his collection of more than 70,000 objects (coins, medals, shells, paintings, books, manuscripts, and botanical specimens), a library, and herbarium to King George II for the nation in return for the payment of £20,000 to his heirs. Sloane was especially keen to see the collection kept together as a whole, and had the terms of the bequest been declined, it would have been offered to learned academies abroad. There is a 1736 bust of Sloane by Rysbrack to the right of the main entrance. Despite the King's lack of interest, Parliament was persuaded to accept the gift, and an act of Parliament establishing the British Museum received the royal assent on 7 June 1753. The Cotton collection of manuscripts, given to the nation in 1700, was attached to the new museum, and £10,000 went to the purchase of the Harley manuscript collection. In 1802, the museum acquired the Rosetta Stone and other Egyptian antiquities, and in 1816, most controversially, the Elgin Marbles.

The main parts of the building were designed by Robert Smirke between 1823 and 1850. In 1883, the natural history collections were moved to a new building in South Kensington, later to become the Natural History Museum. In 2000, the British Library vacated the Reading Room and moved to St. Pancras. Norman Foster designed the marvellous Great Court, which opened that year, with the great Reading Room at its centre, restored to its original design. In 2003, the 250th anniversary of the museum's foundation, the King's Library was given over to a permanent exhibition of that moment in the Enlightenment era when the museum itself came into being. The British Museum is a vast affair, and its holdings are of an almost unimaginable richness. Its ninety-four galleries stretch over a distance of some two and a half miles, arranged over three floors, with Greece, Rome, and the Ancient Near East represented on all three levels. Other galleries are devoted to Britain and Europe, the Americas, Asia, and Africa.

The Department of Greek and Roman Antiquities has one of the most comprehensive collections of objects from the Classical world, ranging in date from the beginning of the Greek Bronze Age (about 3200 BC) to the reign of the Roman emperor Constantine in the fourth century AD. The Greek collection includes elements of two of the Seven Wonders of the Ancient World—the Mausoleum at Halikarnassos and the Temple of Artemis at Ephesus—as well as important holdings of jewellery and bronzes, Greek vases, and Roman glass and silver. The Department of the Ancient Near East covers those ancient civilizations up to the arrival of Islam in the seventh century AD, with a huge range of archaeological material and ancient art, including Assyrian reliefs, Phoenician ivories, and the library of cuneiform tablets from Nineveh.

On the lower floor, the Sainsbury African Galleries contain one of the finest collections of African art and artefacts in the world, comprising 200,000 objects that range from textiles and weaponry to Asante goldwork from Ghana and the Torday collection of Central African sculpture. A key area of the Asian holdings is the most extensive collection in the world of sculpture from the Indian subcontinent as well as an outstanding collection of Chinese antiquities: paintings, porcelain, lacquer, bronze, and jade. There is a remarkable collection of Buddhist paintings from Central Asia and a broad range of Islamic pottery, paintings, tiles, metalwork, glass, seals, and inscriptions. The Japanese Section keeps one of the most comprehensive collections of Japanese material culture in Europe, particularly rich in prints and printed books, paintings, ceramics, swords, decorative arts, and early archaeological material.

Also on the main floor are the galleries devoted to the Americas, including a significant gathering of pre-Hispanic artefacts from the Aztec and Mayan periods and a notable holding of Mixtec-Aztec turquoise mosaics. A gallery displaying Egyptian sculpture has been part of the museum since the very earliest days. With the exception of a group of star objects, including the Rosetta Stone, at the entrance to the gallery, the present arrangement runs chronologically from south to north. Funerary objects are placed in their original tomb contexts, helping to explain the background and significance of the individual elements of burials. The displays make extensive use of modern research methods such as X-rays and CAT scans.

On the upper floor, the collections in the new Department of Prehistory and Europe cover the two million years from the earliest human tools in Africa and Asia to the present day. The department includes the remarkable Waddesdon Bequest, a 300-piece collection of precious objects, assembled in the nineteenth century by two members of the Rothschild family and bequeathed to the museum in 1898. The bequest includes pieces from famous collections such as the Holy Thorn Reliquary belonging to Jean, Duc du Berry (died 1416).

The Early Medieval Gallery covers the dramatic period between the third and fourth centuries through to the early twelfth: the Anglo-Saxon and Viking cultures, the Celts and early medieval Germanic peoples, Goths, Franks, and Lombards. The exquisite Irish Londesborough brooch, of silver and gold, from the eighth or ninth century, is here, as is the haunting Anglo-Saxon helmet from the ship burial at Sutton Hoo, covered with decorative tinned bronze panels. The Medieval Gallery has the wonderful Lewis Chessmen, as well as metalwork, coins, panel painting, leatherwork and tiles. Other European galleries range from Tudor palaces through the great periods of scientific invention, of trade and discovery, to the Gothic revival.

Also on the upper floor, a subject of general interest: money. The Department of Coins and Medals holds one of the finest collections in the world, a million objects tracing the history of coinage since the seventh century BC. The national collection of paper money is also here, as well as a magnificent selection of medals from the Italian Renaissance to the present. The Department of Prints and Drawings contains the national collection of Western prints and drawings, in the same way that the National and Tate Galleries hold the national collection of paintings. One of the top three collections of its kind in the world, it comprises some 50,000 drawings and over two million prints dating from the beginning of the fifteenth century up to the present day.

In the new Wellcome Trust Gallery, the first of a series of long-term exhibitions that draw on the museum collections — Living and Dying — looks at how people around the world view well-being in individual or community terms and how they seek to avert or confront grief, sickness, and other crises in their lives. A few more highlights of the museum collections, almost randomly drawn from a very long list, might include the decorated Iznik basin from the sixteenth century; the Portland Vase, cameo glass, perhaps 2,000 years old; and the famous fourth-century Great Dish from the Mildenhall Treasure. No visitor to the British Museum should have any difficulty in readily finding highlights of his or her own.

British Optical Association Museum

42 Craven Street, London WC2N 5NG

020 7766 4353

www.college-optometrists.org/college/museum

Open: M–F 9:30 AM–5:00 PM. Closed on public holidays. Phone ahead; prior appointment necessary.

Admission: Free

Underground: Charing Cross

Founded in 1901, this is a collection of nearly 10,000 items relating to the history of ophthalmic optics, the human eye, and visual aids. It includes historic examples of pince-nez, lorgnettes, magnifiers, quizzing glasses, monocles, and more than 2,000 pairs of spectacles. The museum possesses the spectacles of such famous individuals as Dr. Johnson, C. P. Snow, and Dr. Crippen and owns the only known pair of Scarlett-type temple spectacles in the world (c. 1730). The collection of twenty-two oil paintings, recently restored, includes a 1777 portrait by Stephen Elmer of Benjamin Franklin, who lodged a few houses away at number 36. The Print Room displays portraits, caricatures, and satires and features work by Cruikshank and Gillray. There is also an extensive collection of optometric instruments and smaller collections of microscopes, telescopes, and cameras. Other highlights include porcelain eyebaths and an extensive display of glass eye models illustrating external diseases and injuries.

British Postal Museum and Archive

Freeling House, Phoenix Place, London WC1X 0DL
020 7239 2570
www.postalheritage.org.uk.
Archive open: M–W & F, 10:00 AM–5:00 PM; Th, 10:00 AM–7:00 PM; occasional Sa
Admission: Free
Underground: Farringdon/Chancery Lane/King's Cross St. Pancras

This combined archive and museum service opened in 2004, six years after the closure of the former National Postal Museum. The Royal Mail Archive records four centuries of the British postal service, including reports on all Royal Mail activities, uniforms, postal rates, and postal technology; staff records; and maps, posters, and photographs. Unsurprisingly, there is a fine stamp collection, including original artwork and a display of British postal markings from 1661 to the present day. Currently located north-east of London until a new site is found on which both collections can be displayed together, the British Postal Museum Store houses objects ranging from the desk of Rowland Hill (founder of the Penny Post) to Mobile Post Office vehicles and an extensive assortment of letter boxes. The BPMA continues to collect material reflecting the service in the twenty-first century, and a new visitor centre is planned to open in 2009.

Bruce Castle Museum

Church Lane off Lordship Lane, London N17 8NU
020 8808 8772
www.haringey.gov.uk/leisure/brucecastlemuseum

Open: W–Su and summer Bank Holidays, 1:00 PM–5:00 PM. Visiting groups, including schools, may book to visit at other times. The local history archive is open to researchers by appointment.
Admission: Free
Underground: Wood Green

Bruce Castle is a sixteenth-century manor house that has been modified in the seventeenth, eighteenth, and nineteenth centuries. Set in twenty acres of parkland, it houses the borough of Haringey's local history collections, which include photographs, paintings, prints, and drawings and a postal history collection commemorating Sir Rowland Hill, whose family ran a progressive school for boys at Bruce Castle in the Victorian period. Hill reformed the British postal system and famously introduced the Penny Post. Bruce Castle opened as a museum in 1906. Exhibitions cover the history of the local area and Bruce Castle itself. There is a new interactive exhibition devoted to local inventors, and the museum regularly hosts temporary local history and art exhibitions.

Brunel Museum

Railway Avenue, Rotherhithe, London SE16 4LF
020 7231 3840
www.brunelenginehouse.org.uk

🏛 🍽 🔭

Open: Daily, 10:00 AM–5:00 PM
Admission: £2.00; Concessions and children, £1.00
Underground: Rotherhithe

This small museum celebrates the construction of Thames Tunnel, the first tunnel to be constructed under a river. Running from Rotherhithe to Wapping, it was designed and built by Sir Marc Brunel, father of Isambard Kingdom Brunel, who pioneered techniques still used in modern tunnel building. After his father fell ill, Isambard Kingdom Brunel completed the work, his first project. It is still used by the London Underground system today, linking Rotherhithe station with Wapping, on the north bank of the Thames. The museum has a collection of illustrations and models detailing the work of Sir Marc Brunel and the project's many problems over eighteen years (1825–1843), including accidents and floodings. However, the celebrations are also shown, including the banquet held inside the tunnel on 10 November 1827. The Engine House is itself a striking piece of nineteenth-century architecture, a listed red brick building designed by Sir Marc Brunel to contain the steam engines that drained the tunnel.

Buckingham Palace

London SW1A 1AA Ticket office at Visitor Entrance, Buckingham
Palace Road
www.royalcollection.org.uk

Open: Daily, 9:45 AM–6:00 PM, 28 July–25 Sept
Admission: State Rooms, Adult, £15.00; Over 60/Student, £13.00;
Children under 17, £8.50; Children under 5, Free; Family, £38.50.
Combined ticket with Queen's Gallery and Royal Mews (available 28
July–25 September only): Adult, £27.00; Over 60/Student, £24.00;
Children under 17, £15.50; Children under 5, Free; Family, £69.50
Underground: Victoria/St. James's Park

Buckingham Palace is the Queen's official London residence and
evolved from a town house that was owned from the beginning of
the eighteenth century by the Dukes of Buckingham. John Nash
did much of the conversion work for George IV between 1825
and 1830, and many of the furnishings come from Carlton
House, George IV's splendid home at the time. The palace was
still unfinished at the King's death, though, and Victoria was the
first British monarch to live here. Although in use for many official events and receptions, areas of the palace are opened to visitors during the summer on a regular basis. The state rooms are
furnished with some of the greatest treasures from the Royal collection—the Picture Gallery (Nash's design) features paintings by
Rembrandt, Rubens, Poussin, van Dyck, and Canaletto; the
sculpture in the Marble Hall, built by Nash for just that purpose,
includes several works by Antonio Canova; the Sèvres porcelain
on show includes the table made for Napoleon, situated now in
the Blue Drawing Room, with its thirty fake onyx columns; and
some of the world's finest English and French furniture.

Burgh House & The Hampstead Museum

New End Square, Hampstead, London NW3 1LT

020 7431 0144

www.burghhouse.org.uk

Open: W–Su, noon–5:00 PM; Sa, by appointment only; Bank Holidays, 2:00 PM–5:00 PM; closed Christmas week.

Admission: Free

Underground: Hampstead

Burgh House is a fine Queen Anne (1704) building in the heart of old Hampstead. The Hampstead Museum, occupying the first floor of the house, specializes in the local history of the area, with displays ranging from prehistoric to modern times. Celebrated Hampstead residents have included John Constable and the watercolourist Helen Allingham, some of whose work is always on display here. She was married to the Irish poet and diarist William Allingham, who knew an extraordinary number of Victorian literary notables. Other occupants of the house have included Thomas Grylls, who designed the rose window above Poet's Corner in Westminster Abbey; Dr. George Williamson, an international art expert, who commissioned Gertrude Jekyll to design the garden here (only the terrace remains); and Elsie Bambridge, the daughter of Rudyard Kipling, whose last outing in 1936 was to visit her. Burgh House escaped serious bomb damage during the Second World War; it was bought and restored by Hampstead Borough Council in 1946.

Cabinet War Rooms

Clive Steps, King Charles Street, London SW1A 2AQ
020 7930 6961
http://cwr.iwm.org.uk/

Open: 9:30 AM–6:00 PM (last admission 5:00 PM); closed 24–26 Dec.
Admission: £11.00; Concessions, £9.00; Children under 16, Free; Disabled visitors, £6.00; Carers, Free. Includes admission to Churchill Museum.
Underground: Westminster

This network of rooms beneath the Government Office Building is where the War Cabinet met more than a hundred times during the Second World War, first under Neville Chamberlain, then, following his resignation, under Winston Churchill, who became Prime Minister in May 1940. They include living quarters for senior ministers, the Map Room, and the office from which Churchill made broadcasts and conducted meetings with heads of state, politicians, and military leaders. The Map Room came into use on the very first day that the Cabinet War Rooms were ready for occupation and never ceased to be the hub of the whole site until VJ Day. A new addition is the Churchill Museum, the first national museum dedicated to Winston Churchill, which presents both public and private portraits. From the young Churchill through his early political career, the wilderness years, and his emergence as war leader, the displays are impressively reinforced by the interactive lifeline table, which brings up a wealth of contextual material, text, visual images, and sound, at a touch.

Carlyle's House

24 Cheyne Row, Chelsea, London SW3 5HL

020 7352 7087

www.nationaltrust.org.uk/carlyleshouse

Open: W–F, 2:00 PM–5:00 PM, Mar–Oct; Sa, Su, and Bank Holiday
Mondays, 11:00 AM–5:00 PM (last admission 4:30 PM)

Admission: £4.50; Child, £2.30; Guided tours, for groups outside normal hours, £5.50: please phone to arrange.

Underground: Sloane Square/South Kensington

Thomas Carlyle and his wife Jane lived in this Queen Anne
house from 1834 to 1881. They initially took just a year's renew-
able lease, which continued until 1852, when they made a more
permanent agreement. In all that time, the couple paid only
£35.00 a year in rent; they never owned the house. It was here,
in his study at the top of the house, that Carlyle wrote his
biographies of Cromwell and Frederick the Great and his
hugely influential history of the French Revolution, published
in 1837. Such Victorian luminaries as Tennyson and Browning
were visitors, as were Darwin, Dickens, and Emerson. Jane
Carlyle died in 1866, but Thomas Carlyle ("the Sage of
Chelsea") lived on in the house until his own death in 1881.
Fourteen years later, the house was purchased by public subscription and a memorial trust was formed to administer the
house. The responsibility for the house's upkeep became the
National Trust's in 1936. Many original features survive, and the
house contains much of the Carlyles' furniture, as well as books,
pictures, and personal possessions. There is a small walled garden, much as it was in Carlyle's time, where his dog, Nero, is
buried.

Cartoon Museum

35 Little Russell Street, London WC1A 2HH
020 7580 8155
www.cartoonmuseum.org

Open: Tu–Sa, 10:30 AM–5:30 PM; Su, noon–5:30 PM
Admission: £3.00; Concessions, £2.00; Students and children under 18, Free
Underground: Tottenham Court Road

The Cartoon Museum, opened in February 2006, intends to preserve and present the best of British cartoons, caricatures, comics, and animation. On the ground floor, the Calman Gallery hosts temporary exhibitions while there is a permanent display of the History of Cartoons and Caricature, ranging from classic works by Gillray, Rowlandson, Hogarth, and Cruikshank through the period of H. M. Bateman, Donald McGill, and Heath Robinson to contemporary political cartoonists Steve Bell and Gerald Scarfe. The history of comics and cartoon strips on the first floor features some rare and original artwork on loan from such legendary comics as The Beano, The Dandy, and The Topper, featuring The Bash Street Kids, Roger the Dodger, Desperate Dan, Beryl the Peril, and Dennis the Menace. From an earlier era, the display of classic war cartoons includes Sir David Low and Bruce Bairnsfather. Over the two floors, there are more than 250 original cartoons. The Young Artists' Gallery has facilities for drawing and learning about cartoons, and the Heneage Library's 4,000 volumes are available, by appointment, for browsing and research. There is also a dedicated comics library upstairs.

Charles Dickens Museum

48 Doughty Street, London WC1N 2LX
020 7405 2127
www.dickensmuseum.com
Open: M–Sa, 10:00 AM–5:00 PM (last admission 4:30 PM); Su, 11:00
AM–5:00 PM; closed 25 Dec. and 1 Jan.
Admission: £5.00; Concessions, £4.00; Children, £3.00
Underground: Chancery Lane/Russell Square

Dickens lived in this house for two and a half years, from the
spring of 1837 to the end of 1839, during which time two of his
daughters were born and he worked on *Pickwick Papers*, *Oliver
Twist*, and *Nicholas Nickleby*, among other projects. The house
was bought by the Dickens Fellowship in 1924 and opened as a
museum in the following year. It is still recognizably a family
home, though packed with Dickens memorabilia of all sorts,
from manuscripts and jewellery to furniture and portraits, and
items brought from Dickens' other houses. The drawing room
was restored as far as possible to its 1839 state a little over twenty years ago, while the morning room contains wedding portraits of both Dickens and Catherine by Samuel Laurence.
Among other highlights is the original little wooden midship-
man, prominent in *Dombey and Son*. It was the trade-sign of
the nautical instrument makers Norie and Wilson and was
deposited in the museum on permanent loan just after the
Second World War. Also here is *Dickens's Dream*, the well-
known painting by Robert Buss of Dickens sitting in his study
at Gad's Hill, dreaming of some of the characters he created.
It was donated by the artist's grandson in 1931.

Chartered Insurance Institute Museum

20 Aldermanbury, London EC2V 7HY

020 7417 4417

www.24hourmuseum.org.uk

Open: M–F, 9:00 AM–5:00 PM by appointment only; closed Bank
Holidays. Normally open during office hours, but visitors should ring in
advance.

Admission: Free

Underground: Bank/ Moorgate/St. Paul's

Fire insurance came into being in the aftermath of the Great
Fire of London, which devastated more than one-third of the
city. The only compensation hitherto available for victims of
disaster came from collections at the local church. Since many
streets were unnamed and the houses unnumbered, insurance
companies issued firemarks that their clients had to display on
the outside of their buildings to show that they had purchased
cover. This small museum has an unrivalled collection of these
firemarks and fireplates on display, together with a variety of
other artefacts relating to the history of firefighting and fire
insurance.

Chelsea FC Centenary Museum

Chelsea Football Club, Stamford Bridge, London SW6 1HS
Tel: 0870 300 1212
www.chelseafc.com
Open: M–F, 10:30 AM–4:30 PM, Sa–Su, 11:30 AM–4:00 PM; the
museum will not be open on home match days.
Admission: £5.00; Concessions, £3.00
Underground: Fulham Broadway

Chelsea Football Club opened its Centenary Museum in 2005
to commemorate the founding of the club. It pays tribute to
the last hundred years of the Stamford Bridge side, with a host
of exhibits, sights, and sounds. The museum is divided into
decades, with each period illustrating how the club fared while
also setting its achievements into the context of contemporary
events. There is a growing collection of memorabilia, ranging
from Seamus O'Connell's England caps and medals to Roy
Bentley's boots and manager José Mourinho's trademark
Armani coat.

Chelsea Physic Garden

Swan Walk, London SW3 4HS
020 7352 5646
www.chelseaphysicgarden.co.uk

Open: Su and Bank Holidays, noon–6:00 PM; W, noon–dusk or 9:00
PM (whichever is earlier), Apr–Oct; Th and F, noon–5:00 PM
Admission: Adults and senior citizens, £7.00; Students, unemployed
people, and children 5 to 15 years old, £4.00; Companions for dis-
abled visitors, Free
Underground: Sloane Square

The Chelsea Physic Garden became a registered charity and
opened to the general public for the first time in 1983. It was
founded by the Society of Apothecaries in 1673 to train
apprentices in plant identification and to promote the study of
botany in relation to medicine, then known as the "physic," or
healing, arts. The riverside location offered both a convenient
means of transport and slightly milder weather conditions in
which nonnative plants might better withstand the English
winters. In 1712, Dr. Hans Sloane, after whom the nearby locations of Sloane Square and Sloane Street were named, purchased the Manor of Chelsea and, ten years later, leased this
plot of around four acres to the Society of Apothecaries for
£5.00 a year in perpetuity. A statue of Sloane still stands in the
centre of the garden. The oldest rock garden in England on
view to the public was completed here in 1773, constructed
from a variety of rock types, including stones from the Tower
of London and Icelandic lava (brought to the garden by Sir
Joseph Banks in 1772 on a ship named St. Lawrence). Until the
mid-nineteenth century, most medicines were derived from

herbs, plants, and vegetables. The Physic Garden thus served as a place of instruction, in addition to providing simples and raw materials for the manufacture of drugs in the laboratory at Apothecaries' Hall. This, the second oldest botanic garden in England, still fulfils its traditional functions of scientific research and plant conservation. Its aims include displaying the range of plant species introduced to Britain by a succession of famous curators, pursuing horticultural excellence, and demonstrating to all its visitors the many uses of plants, particularly showing countless examples of medicinal plants gathered from all over the world.

Chiswick House

Burlington Lane, Chiswick London W4 2RP
020 8995 0508
www.english-heritage.org.uk/

Open: W–Su, 10:00 AM–5:00 PM (Sa, until 2:00 PM), 1 Apr–31 Oct;
Bank Holidays, 10:00 AM–5:00 PM; 1 Nov–20 Mar, by appointment
only; closed 24 Dec–28 Feb
Admission: £4.20; Concessions, £3.20; Child, £2.10; Family ticket,
£10.50
Underground: Turnham Green

A celebrated example of eighteenth-century British architecture, Chiswick House was designed as his country residence by
the third Earl of Burlington (1694–1753), an enthusiastic admir-
er of the Palladian style and of Inigo Jones, who had pioneered
it in Britain. There are statues of both Palladio and Jones in the
garden. The villa was originally connected to the main house,
being used to store and display Burlington's art collection. Both
the house and the garden, with its classical statuary, draw on the
models of ancient Rome and the Renaissance, and much of the
interior work was carried out by William Kent. The house has
benefited from an extended course of restoration, following a
period of nearly forty years in which it was used as a private
sanatorium. There are many paintings and prints providing an
insight into the Burlington family, and a double portrait of Lord
and Lady Burlington, by William Aikman, hangs alongside
paintings of their two young daughters. Alexander Pope was a
close friend of Burlington and addressed his fourth epistle, full
of architectural references, to him.

Church Farmhouse Museum

Greyhound Hill, Hendon, NW4 4JR
020 8359 3942
www.churchfarmhousemuseum.co.uk
Open: M–Th, 10:00 AM–1:00 PM, 2:00 PM–5:00 PM; Sa, 10:00
AM–1:00 PM, 2:00 PM–5:30 PM; Su, 2:00 PM–5:30 PM; closed on
Fridays.
Admission: Free
Underground: Hendon Central (Northern Line)
Bus: 113, 143, 183, 186, 326

One of the oldest surviving dwellings in the area, Church
Farm was built around 1660. Dairy farming continued here
until the late 1930s, although the character of Hendon had
largely changed from rural to urban a quarter of a century earlier. Hendon Borough Council bought the farmhouse and out-
buildings, together with the adjoining land, in 1944, using the
house to accommodate families whose homes had been damaged or destroyed in the Second World War. The farmhouse
opened as a museum in 1955 and, in addition to a thriving programme of temporary exhibitions, features three distinctive
period rooms. The 1820s kitchen has a huge open fireplace, a
fine oak dresser and a bread oven, as well as an extraordinary
collection of Victorian utensils, while the scullery's display of
laundry equipment includes washing dollies and a linen press.
The 1850s dining room, which boasts an impressive oval dining
table, Windsor chairs, and some highly distinctive oak panelling, is decorated every December for a Victorian Christmas.

Clink Prison Museum

1 Clink Street, London SE1 9DG

020 7403 0900

www.clink.co.uk

Open: Daily, 10:00 AM–9:00 PM (Jun–Sep) and 10:00 AM–6:00 PM (Oct–May); closed 25 Dec.

Admission: £5.00; Concessions, £3.50; Family ticket (2 adults, 2 children), £12.00

Underground: London Bridge

The Clink Museum is on the site of the original prison of that name, which functioned from the twelfth century until 1780, when it was destroyed during the Gordon Riots. The prison, one of the country's oldest as well as the first in which women prisoners were held, was attached to Winchester House, the palace of the Bishops of Winchester, until the seventeenth century, since the surrounding area was under the Bishop's jurisdiction. The prison's inmates tended to include a significant proportion of drunks and prostitutes as well as debtors and prisoners of conscience. The museum reconstructs the prison cells, and its displays include devices of torture and restraint, histories of prostitution and this area of Southwark, notorious for its riotous street life.

The Clockmakers Museum

The Clock Room, Guildhall Library, Aldermanbury, London EC2P 2EJ
020 7332 1868
www.clockmakers.info/index.html

Open: M–Sa, 9:30 AM–4:30 PM; closed on public holidays and the
Saturdays before Bank Holiday Mondays (and, briefly, from time to time
for rewinding and adjusting the clocks).
Admission: Free
Underground: Bank

The Clockmakers' collection is the oldest collection specifically
of clocks and watches in the world and has been on permanent
public display since 1874. The collection is shown in one large
room and comprises some 600 English and European watches,
clocks, and marine timekeepers, as well as horological portraits,
including Holbein's depiction of Nicholas Kratzer. For the
most part, the items date from around 1600 to the mid-nineteenth century. There is work by Edward East, who became
clockmaker to Charles II at the beginning of "the golden age
of English clock making" and by Thomas Tompion, "father of
English clock making," who introduced the balance spring for
watches. Among the notable marine timekeepers are a 1724
piece by Henry Sully, the silver deck watch by Thomas
Earnshaw that Captain George Vancouver used when taking
part in the European discovery of the Island now bearing his
name, and the historically crucial fifth marine timekeeper made
by John Harrison and completed in 1770. A huge circular floor
plaque traces the names—and distances from the site at which
they worked—of scores of London clockmakers over three
centuries.

The Clowns Gallery and Museum

The All Saints Centre, Haggerston Road, London E8 4HT

0870 1284336

www.clowns-international.co.uk

Open: First F afternoon of every month from noon–5:00 PM. Parties should advise the manager in advance to arrange alternative visiting days.

Admission: Free, but donations always welcome.

Underground: Nearest station is Dalston Kingsland, reached via Silverlink from Highbury and Islington underground. Or London Fields from Liverpool Street.

Buses: 30, 38, 67, 73, 76, 149, 236, 242, 243. There is then a short walk to the museum.

The Clowns Museum was founded in 1960 by Clowns International and provides a national showcase for the international history of clowns and clowning. There is a wide variety of exhibits on show, including costumes, props, photographs, posters, prints, and paintings. In addition there is the famous collection of painted pot eggs accurately representing the "slap" (facial makeup) of real clowns, plus all sorts of clown memorabilia. There is an audiovisual corner showing live clowning and a small library archive of clown-related literature. The earliest exhibits are around 200 years old, and displays of contemporary clown images are constantly updated. The collection was previously housed at the nearby Holy Trinity Church, in Beechwood Road, Dalston, where the Joseph Grimaldi memorial service is held annually on the first Sunday in February.

Cuming Museum

151 Walworth Road, London SE17 1RY

020 7525 2332

www.southwark.gov.uk/DiscoverSouthwark/Museums/TheCumingMuseum

Open: Tu–Sa, 10:00 AM–5:00 PM; closed Su, M, and Bank Holidays.

Admission: Free

Underground: Elephant and Castle

A gift of three fossils and an Indian coin from his aunt apparently launched Richard Cuming (1777–1870) upon his lifelong devotion to collecting, beginning with shells and rocks, then extending to other areas of science and natural history. His son Henry Syer Cuming shared his interests but was also fascinated by the history and archaeology of South London. Between them, they amassed a collection of more than 100,000 objects from dozens of countries, from Egyptian artefacts to theatre posters, though without travelling themselves, since they bought mostly from London auction houses. Henry Cuming bequeathed the collection to the Metropolitan Borough of Southwark when he died in 1902. It was to be known as the Cuming Museum, and he left a sum of money to employ a curator. Opened in 1906 by Lord Rothschild, the museum remained in the same gallery for a hundred years and, to mark that anniversary, moved to a new home in the Walworth Town Hall Building in October 2006. There are permanent exhibitions devoted to the Cumings and the evolution of their extraordinary collection and to the history of Southwark.

Cutty Sark Clipper Ship

King William Walk, Greenwich, London SE10 9HT
020 8858 3445
www.cuttysark.org.uk

Open: Daily, 10:00 AM–5:00 PM; closed 24–26 Dec.
Admission: £5.00; Concessions £3.90; Children under 16, £3.70;
Children under 5, Free
Train: Cutty Sark on DLR (Docklands Light Railway)

The *Cutty Sark* is the only surviving example of the tea clippers, the great ships that raced to bring back the new season's tea from the Far East. Launched in 1869 at Dumbarton, the *Cutty Shark* made eight voyages to China and, when fourteen years old, achieved a return passage time from Australia of eighty-three days, the best of the year. Bought and restored as a tea clipper by Wilfred Dowman in 1922, the *Cutty Sark* was opened to the public and used as a cadet training ship. After taking part in the 1951 Festival of Britain celebrations, she was towed into a specially constructed dry dock and has remained there ever since. Officially opened after restoration by the Queen in 1957, the ship received fifteen million visitors by the end of 2006.

A major restoration project began in November 2006, scheduled to last until October 2008, with a new, adjoining visitor centre pavilion displaying a history of the *Cutty Sark* and details of the project. At the time of publication, a devastating fire has inflicted major damage on the ship's structure and the prospects of eventual restoration are still being assessed by the *Cutty Sark* Trust.

Czech Memorial Scrolls Centre

Kent House, Rutland Gardens, London SW7 1BX (Kent House is at the corner of Rutland Gardens and Knightsbridge, opposite Knightsbridge Barracks)

020 7584 3741 (Tu and Th, 10:00 AM–4:00 PM)

www.czechmemorialscrollstrust.org

Open: Tu and Th, 10:00 AM–4:00 PM

Admission: Free, but donations welcome and urgently needed.

Underground: Knightsbridge

Bus: 9, 10, 52

The Czech Memorial Scrolls Trust was responsible for rescuing the collection of nearly 2,000 Torah Scrolls and Torah Binders included among the ritual objects that were accumulated during the Nazi occupation of Bohemia and Moravia in Czechoslovakia and stored in a Prague synagogue. The collection was purchased with the help of the art dealer and collector Eric Estorick and arrived in London in 1964. Over the next thirty years, the trust undertook the restoration and distribution of the scrolls across the world. The exhibition illustrates the extraordinary story of the scrolls, illuminating the history of the Jewish communities of Bohemia and Moravia, the rescue of the scrolls from the deserted synagogues, and their postwar discovery, repair, and distribution. It also recounts the more recent events in the story, detailing the return of scrolls to Jewish life all over the world as valued memorials to the vanished communities and the people who belonged to them.

Dalí Universe

County Hall, Westminster Bridge Road, London SE1 7PB
020 7967 8000
www.daliuniverse.com

Open: 10:00 AM–6:30 PM, last admission 5:30 PM
Admission: £12.00; Concessions, £10; Children, 8–16, £8.00;
Children, 4–7, £5.00; Children under 4, Free
Underground: Waterloo

The Dalí Universe has over 500 works by Salvador Dalí,
including paintings and graphics, drawings, and, particularly,
sculpture. The collection is the most extensive in the world,
covering half a century from 1935 to 1984. There are also gold
and glass objects and a Dalí-inspired furniture collection. The
collection, curated by Dalí's friend, Beniamino Levi, includes
major Dalí works such as the Mae West Lips Sofa, Lobster
Telephone, and *Spellbound*, the large canvas commissioned by
Alfred Hitchcock for his 1945 film of the same name. All the
main themes of Dalí's life and work — dreams and the subcon-
scious, his relations with the church, eroticism — are addressed
here.

De Morgan Centre

38 West Hill, Wandsworth, London SW18 1RZ
020 8871 1144
www.demorgan.org.uk

Open: Tu–W, noon–6:00 PM; F–Sa, 10:00 AM–5:00 PM; closed
Sundays, Mondays, and Thursdays.
Admission: Free
Underground: East Putney

Located in what was the reading room of the adjoining West
Hill Reference Library, the De Morgan Centre contains the
largest single collection of work by the Victorian ceramic artist
William De Morgan: plates, pottery, and tiles. It also holds the
world's primary collection of work by his wife, the painter
Evelyn De Morgan, together with an archive of papers relating
to their lives, and a temporary exhibition space. One of the most
celebrated nineteenth-century ceramicists, long associated with
William Morris, for whose firm he designed stained glass and
tiles, William De Morgan's most recognizable quality as a potter
is that curious opalescence resulting from his rediscovery of the
technique of lustre. His researches were stimulated by his intense
admiration for the bright turquoise on the sixteenth-century
Isnik work that he saw at the recently opened South Kensington
Museum (later the V & A Museum). De Morgan's achievements in the design of such turquoise tiles are displayed to bril-
liant effect in the Frederic Leighton House. He also became a
bestselling novelist late in life. Evelyn De Morgan, one of the
first female students at the Slade School of Art, became a highly
successful painter, influenced both by the Pre-Raphaelites and by
the Renaissance Old Masters whom she studied in Italy.

Dennis Severs' House

18 Folgate Street, London E1 6BX
020 7247 4013
www.dennissevershouse.co.uk

Open: Every Monday except Bank Holidays; after dark, by candlelight:
"Silent Night," booking necessary; first and third Su, noon–4:00 PM,
booking not necessary; lunchtime, noon–4:00 PM on the Mondays fol-
lowing the first and third Sundays, no booking necessary.
Admission: "Silent Night," £12,00; First and third Sundays, £8.00;
Mondays following, £5.00
Underground: Liverpool Street

This Georgian terraced house is a living museum set up by
American-born Dennis Severs, who died in 1999, and tells the
story of the Jarvis family, a fictional group of Huguenot silk
weavers living in Spitalfields from 1725 to the First World War.
The remarkable journey, through ten rooms from kitchen to
attic and nearly two centuries, from the family's arrival to the
collapse of the silk industry and beyond, was created over
twenty years as Severs furnished the house from local markets
and redecorated rooms in the style of the period. The house
motto is "You either see it or you don't," and the tour of the
house comprises a series of tableaux vivants, experienced ideally
by candlelight—and in silence—an experience heightened by
shadows, sounds, and smells: horses' hooves on the cobbles
outside, footsteps and whispers, clocks and creaks, and the
strong sensation of the house's inhabitants having just that
moment slipped away, leaving bread broken on the table and a
kettle hissing on the hob.

Design Museum

28 Shad Thames, Butlers Wharf, London SE1 2YD
0870 833 9955
www.designmuseum.org

Open: Daily, 10:00 AM–5:45 PM (last admission 5:15 PM); closed 25 and 26 Dec.
Admission: £7.00; Concessions, £4.00; Under 12, Free
Underground: Tower Hill/London Bridge

The Design Museum was founded in 1989 by Sir Terence Conran as the first dedicated museum of contemporary, particularly industrial, design. Set in a beautifully converted 1940s warehouse, it has superb views over the Thames. In addition to its temporary exhibitions of contemporary design and design history, there is a permanent collection devoted to notable product designs, concentrating on mass-produced articles and their manufacturers as well as their designers. These range from desk lamps to computers and include examples of cars, electronic equipment, tableware, textiles, and, particularly, office and domestic furniture. One outstanding feature is the extraordinary range of examples of the design of the chair, including items by Mies van der Rohe, Marcel Breuer, Charles and Ray Eames, Jasper Morrison, and Alvar Aalto. The review collection holds state of the art innovations from around the world.

Dr. Johnson's House

17 Gough Square, London EC4 A 3DE
020 7353 3745
www.drjohnsonshouse.org

Open: M–Sa, 11:00 AM–5:30 PM (until 5:00 PM in winter, Oct–Apr);
closed public holidays.
Admission: £4.50; Concessions, £3.50; Children, £1.50. Pre-booked
guided tours—and evening tours—are available for groups.
Underground: Blackfriars/Temple/Chancery Lane/Holborn

Gough Square stands within a network of walkways and pas-
sages. Samuel Johnson lived here from 1748 to 1759 (partly
because it was close to the printer, William Strahan), devoting
much of that time to his enormous undertaking of the first
comprehensive dictionary of the English Language (he became
known as "Dictionary Johnson"). His wife's death in 1752
affected him profoundly, but the dictionary was published in
1755, and first editions are included in the house's collection of
books, prints, portraits, mezzotints, and letters. In the garret of
the house, six copyists stood and transcribed the dictionary
entries while Johnson pored over other books, marking the
words he wished to include. The house was rescued from demolition in 1911 by Cecil, later Lord, Harmsworth and opened
to the public in the following year. It has now been restored to
its eighteenth-century condition and period furniture carefully
obtained and added to the house, including pieces which
belonged to Johnson's friend Mrs. Carter. Highlights include
the Wedgwood medallion of Johnson and a self-portrait by Sir
Joshua Reynolds.

Dulwich Picture Gallery

Gallery Road, Dulwich, London SE21 7AD
020 8693 5254
www.dulwichpicturegallery.org.uk

Open: Tu–F, 10:00 AM–5:00 PM; Sa, Su, and Bank Holiday Mondays, 11:00 AM–5:00 PM
Admission: Permanent collection, £4.00; Senior citizens, £3.00; Unemployed, Disabled, Students, and Children, Free
Train: North Dulwich (from London Bridge); West Dulwich (from Victoria)

The Dulwich is the oldest public art gallery in the country. Designed by Sir John Soane (1811–1813) and purpose-built to display pictures, it opened its doors to the public in 1817, seven years before the National Gallery. The irresistible story of the collection includes the central fact of its having originally been assembled for the King of Poland. More immediately, the gallery's holdings are based on the 1811 bequest of over 350 Old Masters from Sir Francis Bourgeois. Further galleries were added around 1910. Internally, the gallery has been restored as far as possible to its original appearance. The holdings of British pictures are largely from Charles Fairfax Murray's bequests (1911 to 1919). Among the many highlights of the collection, which is particularly strong in seventeenth- and eighteenth-century European artists, are paintings by Claude, Poussin, and Watteau; a fine showing of Dutch and Flemish art, including work by Albert Cuyp and Jacob van Ruisdael; Rembrandt's *Girl at a Window* and Murillo's *Flower Girl*. There are several works by Veronese, more than a dozen Van Dycks, and nine by Reynolds. Among the examples of Gainsborough's art is *The Linley Sisters*.

Fan Museum

12 Croom's Hill, London SE10 8ER
020 8858 7879
www.fan-museum.org/collection.asp

Open: Tu–Sa, 11:00 AM–5:00 PM; Su, noon–5:00 PM
Admission: £4.00; Concessions, £3.00; Children under 7, free
Train: to Greenwich from Charing Cross; Cutty Sark (DLR)

Devoted to every aspect of the history of fans and fan making, this is the only museum of its kind in the world, housed in a striking pair of listed Georgian buildings. The core of the whole enterprise is the outstanding Hélène Alexander collection, numbering some 2,000 items, which has been augmented, since the museum's founding in 1991, by many gifts and bequests. The total holdings of fans and fan leaves now total around 3,500, from the eleventh century to the present, and taking in fans from all over the world. The museum is, though, particularly strong in eighteenth- and nineteenth-century European fans. It has recently acquired an outstanding fan, painted in gouache on vellum by Walter Sickert around 1889, which portrays the music-hall artiste Little Dot Hetherington on stage at a Camden theatre. The museum's permanent exhibition is an introduction to the history of fans, the techniques and types and materials involved in fan making. The second exhibition changes three times a year, usually highlighting a particular theme and enabling more examples from this prestigious collection to be shown. Afternoon teas are served in the Orangery on Tuesdays and Sundays from 3:00 PM.

Faraday Museum

The Royal Institution, 21 Albemarle Street, London W1S 4BS
020 7409 2992
www.rigb.org

Open: Currently closed; call for updated information
Admission: Call for information
Underground: Green Park

The Faraday Museum, devoted to the great experimental physicist and chemist Michael Faraday (1791–1867), features his reconstructed laboratory together with a display of personal effects and scientific apparatus.

At the time of writing, the museum is closed to the public due to an ambitious scheme of development and refurbishment. The design proposals provide for several new public spaces, including a café and restaurant, and the pièce de résistance: a magnificent day-lit atrium. The collections in the Michael Faraday Museum and the archives will be undergoing major reinterpretation during this period, and when the building reopens, there will be new display areas across the lower three floors. These will exhibit the work of other great scientists such as Humphry Davy, James Dewar, William Bragg, and Lawrence Bragg to the public for the very first time at exhibition standards.

Fenton House

20 Hampstead Grove, Windmill Hill, Hampstead, London NW3 6RT
020 7435 3471
www.nationaltrust.org.uk/fentonhouse

Open: W–F, 2:00 PM–5:00 PM; Sa–Su, 11:00 AM–5:00 PM (Apr–Oct)
Admission: House & garden, £5.20; Children, £2.60; Family, £12.50;
Groups, £4.30 per person; Joint ticket with 2 Willow Road (see separate entry), £7.00. Garden only: £2.00; Children, £1.00
Underground: Hampstead

Fenton House, built by a wealthy merchant in the late seventeenth century but named for a much later owner, contains an outstanding collection of English and continental porcelain, particularly Meissen, as well as a fine display of Chinese ware. Also featured are seventeenth-century needlework pictures and Georgian furniture. The other major focal point is the Benton Fletcher collection of early keyboard instruments, most of them in working order and often used: harpsichords, clavichords, virginals, spinets, and pianos. Several of the larger pieces are placed on the lower floors; the rest reside in the attic rooms. The many notable paintings include works by Jan Breugel and G. F. Watts, and there is an early print of Albrecht Dürer's *The Sea Monster*. Also here is a collection of paintings by Sir William Nicholson, currently on loan to the house. They include *Hawking*, a portrait of the artist's son, the painter Ben Nicholson as a boy; and *Nancy*, a portrait of his eldest daughter, who later married the writer Robert Graves. There is a very attractive walled garden and an orchard over 300 years old.

Firepower

The Royal Artillery Museum, The Royal Arsenal, Woolwich, London
SE18 6ST
020 8855 7755
www.firepower.org.uk

🍽️

Open: W–Su and Bank Holidays, 10:30 AM–5:00 PM (Apr–Oct); F–Su
and Bank Holidays, 10:30 AM–5:00 PM (Nov–Mar)
Admission: £5.00; Concessions, £4.50; Children, £2.50
Train: Woolwich Arsenal (from Charing Cross)

The museum exhibits Europe's widest variety of historic and
modern artillery, covering some 600 years of development in
half a dozen galleries. Field of Fire uses smoke, sound effects,
giant film screens, and lights to convey the experience of modern gunnery to the visitor. The History Gallery's story of
weaponry details Roger Bacon's thirteenth-century rediscovery
of gunpowder and includes among its exhibits the medieval
English siege weapon recovered from the moat at Bodiam
Castle in Sussex. As well as an early British Maxim machine
gun, there is Colt's Gatling gun, dated to the close of the
American Civil War. Gunnery Hall displays more recent
artillery pieces while other galleries offer audiovisual and hands-
on displays and demonstrations, and an exhibition of the extensive collection of medals awarded to members of the Royal
Artillery regiment across its history.

Fleming Collection

13 Berkeley Street, London W1J 8DU
020 7409 5730
www.flemingcollection.co.uk

Open: Tu–Sa, 10:00 AM–5:30 PM
Admission: Free
Underground: Green Park

The Fleming Collection — named after Robert Fleming, born in Dundee in 1845, the founder of Flemings, the former merchant bank — consists of works by numerous prominent Scottish artists from 1770 to the present day. The bulk of it is twentieth century, but it includes works by early nineteenth-century artists, the Glasgow Boys, the Scottish Colourists, the Edinburgh School, and many contemporary Scottish names. Two paintings, *Lochaber No More* by John Watson Nicol (1856–1926) and *The Last of the Clan* by Thomas Faed (1826–1900), have become probably the most familiar images of the Highland Clearances. The present gallery opened to the public in January 2002 and holds regular exhibitions drawn from the collection as well as loans from public and private collections of Scottish art.

Florence Nightingale Museum

2 Lambeth Palace Road, London SE1 7EH

020 7620 0374

www.florence-nightingale.co.uk

Open: M–F, 10:00 AM–5:00 PM; Sa, Su, and public holidays, 10:00 AM–4:30 PM (last admission one hour before closing); closed 23 Dec–2 Jan, Good Friday, Easter Saturday, and Easter Sunday.

Admission: £5.80; Concessions, £4.80

Underground: Waterloo/Westminster

This small museum celebrates and explores the life and work of Florence Nightingale through memorabilia, the souvenirs that she collected on her travels, and the defining event of the Crimean War. Nightingale was asked by the government to travel to Scutari in Turkey with a team of nurses. Once there, she organized improvements in the appalling conditions, dramatically raised standards of hygiene and patient care, and returned to England a national heroine. Some of the many gifts and honours she received at the time are now on display. She also established the Nightingale Training School of Nursing and was instrumental in effecting crucial developments in midwifery and health visiting. She was generally influential in raising the status and efficiency of nursing, often in the face of fierce opposition from more conservative forces in the medical services. Paintings, prints, letters, drawings, and life-size reconstructions help to bring the period to life.

Foundling Museum

40 Brunswick Square, London WC1N 1AZ
020 7841 3600
www.foundlingmuseum.org.uk

Open: Tu–Sa, 10:00 AM–6:00 PM; Su, noon–6:00 PM
Admission: £5.00; Concessions, £4.00; Children up to 16, Free
Underground: Russell Square

The Foundling Hospital was granted its Royal charter in 1739 and admitted its first foundlings in March 1741. It was begun by Thomas Coram, a retired shipwright, who was appalled by the abandonment of up to a thousand children each year in London. The hospital cared for 27,000 children before its closure in 1953, and the Coram Family charity still runs projects for disadvantaged children while also maintaining its commitment to making art and music available to them. The early involvement of William Hogarth led to the Foundling Hospital effectively becoming the country's first public art gallery, since Hogarth encouraged other painters and sculptors to donate work to the hospital. George Frideric Handel was also an early patron. He conducted several performances of "The Messiah" in the hospital chapel and bequeathed a fair copy of the work to the hospital in his will. As well as a moving history of its primary work, the museum contains an extensive collection of paintings by Reynolds, Gainsborough, and others, in addition to Hogarth. The outstanding Coke collection of Handel memorabilia and manuscript materials is housed on the second floor. Other highlights are Hogarth's great *March to Finchley* and his portrait of Thomas Coram and the remarkable Court Room (completed 1745; reconstructed in 1937).

Freud Museum

20 Maresfield Gardens, London NW3 5SX
020 7435 2002
www.freud.org.uk

Open: W–Su, noon–5:00 PM; closed 24–26 Dec.
Admission: £5.00; Concessions, £3.00; Children under 12, Free
Underground: Finchley Road

The Freud Museum celebrates the life and work of Sigmund Freud and his youngest daughter, Anna. This immensely attractive house was the home of Freud and his family when they escaped the Nazi annexation of Austria in 1938 and remained the family home until Anna's death in 1982. On the ground floor, Freud's study is preserved just as it was during his lifetime. A considerable proportion of his original library is here: apart from medical and psychoanalytical textbooks and monographs, his profound interest in literature is evident in the volumes of Shakespeare, Goethe, Balzac, Heine, and others. The study also contains Freud's extensive collection of Greek, Roman, Oriental, and Egyptian antiquities. He admitted an addiction to collecting and bought many pieces through Vienna auction houses and possessed more than 2,000 pieces by the end of his life. Here, they occupy shelves and cabinets and are even ranged in rows upon Freud's desk. His daughter, Anna, a pioneering psychoanalyst on her own account, particularly with regard to her work with children, lived in the house for over forty years. There is a room devoted to Anna on the upper floor. Also upstairs is a viewing room where visitors can see uniquely fascinating footage of Freud, his family and friends, and prewar Vienna. The Freuds were fortunate enough to be able to bring much of their household effects with them, including some very attractive Austrian painted country furniture. The most famous single item is undoubtedly Freud's couch, long central to his psychoanalytic practice. It is covered with a striking Iranian rug and there are other fine Oriental rugs on the floor and tables. Two portraits of Freud on the landing are worthy of mention: a 1926 sketch by Ferdinand Schmutzer and a drawing by Salvador Dalí, whom Stefan Zweig introduced to Freud in 1938.

Fulham Palace

Bishop's Avenue, London SW6 6EA
020 7736 3233
www.fulhampalace.org

Open: M–Tu, noon–4:00 PM; Sa, 11:00 AM–2:00 PM; Su 11:30
AM–3:30 PM.
Admission: Free
Underground: Putney Bridge

Fulham Palace was the summer residence of the Bishop of
London for over a thousand years, from the eighth century to
the twentieth. The neo-Gothic chapel by William Butterfield
was built in 1866; and a large moat surrounded the Palace until
the early twentieth century. Archaeological excavations have
produced evidence of settlement in Roman and even Neolithic
times here. The twenty-acre botanic gardens are open to the
public and lie to the west and north of Putney Bridge, from
which the annual boat race between Oxford and Cambridge
universities begins. The museum's collections of pictures,
stained glass and archaeological fragments are based in two
rooms in the early nineteenth-century part of the building and
tell the story of the palace. There is also a scale model (1:50)
which shows the building in perfect detail.

Geffrye Museum

Kingsland Road, Shoreditch, London E2 8EA
020 7739 9893
www.geffrye-museum.org.uk

Open: Tu–Sa, 10:00 AM–5:00 PM; Su and Bank Holiday Mondays,
noon–5:00 PM; closed 24–26 Dec, 1 Jan, Good Friday, and non–Bank
Holiday Mondays.
Admission: Free
Underground: Liverpool Street, bus number 149 or 242; Old Street,
bus number 243

The Geffrye Museum displays its fine collections of paintings,
furniture, textiles, and decorative items in a series of period
rooms ranging from 1600 to the present day. Starting with the
Elizabethan and Jacobean Room, the displays lead the visitor
on a walk through time. They demonstrate the changes in taste
and style as manifested in the English domestic interior across
four centuries, from the Stuart room, with its engraved ebony
cabinet made in Paris in 1652 for the diarist John Evelyn,
through the elegant Georgian room, the stylish Victorian interior, the twentieth-century modernity of the 1930s flat, a mid-
century room and late twentieth-century loft living space in a
converted warehouse. The museum is set in eighteenth-century
almshouses with an additional contemporary wing. There is a
delightful walled herb garden and a series of period gardens
reflecting the changes in style from the late Elizabethan to the
Edwardian period.

Golden Hinde Living History Museum

The Golden Hinde, St. Mary Overie Dock, Cathedral Street, London SE1 9DE

Ship office: 020 7403 0123; bookings and information: 0 8700 11 8700

www.goldenhinde.org

Open: Daily, 10:00 AM–5:00 PM; closed 25 Dec, 1 Jan; confirmation advised.

Admission: £6.00; Concessions £4.50; check for group and workshop prices.

Underground: London Bridge

The *Golden Hinde* is a full-scale reconstruction of the famous sixteenth-century warship that travelled over 140,000 miles and in which Sir Francis Drake circumnavigated the world between 1577 and 1580 via the Cape of Good Hope. The following year, Queen Elizabeth I visited the ship and knighted Drake. The ship was berthed on the Thames at Deptford as a memorial to Drake for almost a century, but its timbers finally rotted beyond repair and it was broken up. Today, the only memento is a chair, formed from the remaining sound timber, which was presented to the University of Oxford by Charles II. In its berth near Southwark Cathedral, the *Golden Hinde* is intended to offer visitors the opportunity to experience a sailor's life in the sixteenth century. The ship weighs a little over a hundred tons, has three masts, five levels of deck, including the gun deck, and eighteen cannon. The museum offers guided tours for schools and workshops during the school holidays.

Grant Museum of Zoology & Comparative Anatomy

Darwin Building, University College London, Gower Street, London
WC1E 6BT

020 7679 2647

www.grant.museum.ucl.ac.uk

Open: M–F, 1:00 PM–5:00 PM and other times by appointment; closed
23 Dec–1 Jan

Admission: Free

Underground: Warren Street/Euston Square

The Grant Museum was established in 1827 by Robert Edmond
Grant (1793–1874), the first professor of zoology and compara-
tive anatomy in England, to serve as a teaching collection at the
newly founded University of London (later University College
London). Upon arrival, Grant found no teaching materials with
which to conduct his courses and immediately began to amass
specimens. Many of them are still preserved here, as are specimens collected by T. H. Huxley. Several of the species represented are now endangered or extinct: there are the bones of a
dodo, a complete skeleton of the thylacine (or Tasmanian wolf),
and the skeleton of a quagga. In over 170 years, the museum has
survived ceiling collapses, flooding, threats of closure, and the
evacuation of the entire collection during the Second World
War. In 1997, it was renamed in honour of its founder and continues to be used as a teaching collection, though now accessible
to far more people than ever before. In total, over 30,000 specimens are held, a selection of which is on display at any one
time, including skeletons, mounted animals, and specimens preserved in fluid in Victorian glass cabinets.

Great Ormond Street Hospital Museum

First Floor, 55 Great Ormond Street, London WC1N 3HZ
020 7405 9200 Ext 5920
www.ich.ucl.ac.uk/about_gosh/history/museum.html

Open: M–F, 10:00 AM–4:15 PM (not Bank Holidays) by appointment
only; please telephone first to arrange a visit. Access is by stairs only.
Admission: Free
Underground: Holborn/Russell Square

The Hospital for Sick Children first opened its doors at 49
Great Ormond Street on Valentine's Day, 1852, with ten beds.
Dr. Charles West was the primary force behind its opening,
driven by the shockingly high level of infant mortality in the
capital, at a time when a third of children born in London died
before adulthood. Fundraising dinners were a major part of the
hospital's early promotional activity, and Charles Dickens'
rousing speech at the Freemasons' Hall in 1858 pulled in over
£3,000, enough to buy the house next door and double the
hospital's bed spaces. The new hospital quickly attracted public
support. Queen Victoria and J. M. Barrie, who donated the
copyright to his famous play *Peter Pan* in April 1929 to Great
Ormond Street Hospital for Children, were among the first
eminent figures to pledge their help. The small museum display
includes artefacts, artworks, photographs, and documents out-
lining the history of the hospital.

Guards Museum

Wellington Barracks, Birdcage Walk, London SW1E 6HQ
020 7414 3271
www.theguardsmuseum.com
Open: Daily, 10:00 AM–4:00 PM (last admission 3:30 PM); closed
Christmas period and during official ceremonies.
Admission: £3.00; Concessions, £2.00; Children under 16, Free
Underground: St. James's Park

Opened in 1988, the Guards Museum is beneath the parade
ground of Wellington Barracks, headquarters of the five
Guards regiments: access is from Birdcage Walk. The museum's holdings illustrate the many battles in which the Guards
have engaged, ranging from 1642, during the English Civil War,
to the present. Displays include weapons and an extensive array
of uniforms; a collection of models, trophies, and memorabilia;
and a small exhibition of Victoria Crosses. The museum contains a wealth of information and artefacts pertaining to the five
regiments of Foot Guards; namely Grenadier, Coldstream,
Scots, Irish, and Welsh Guards. Along with the two regiments
of Household Cavalry, they make up Her Majesty's
Household Division and are responsible for guarding the Royal
residences.

Guildhall Art Gallery

Guildhall Yard EC2P 2EJ
020 7332 3700
www.guildhall-art-gallery.org.uk

Open: M–Sa, 10:00 AM–5:00 PM; Su, noon–4:00 PM
Admission: Adults, £2.50; Concessions, £1.00; Children under 16,
Free; All day on Fridays and from 3:30 PM on other days, Free
Underground: Moorgate/Bank

Opened in 1999 (almost sixty years after the original gallery was
burned down during a severe air raid in May 1941), the
Guildhall Art Gallery displays around 250 works of art at a
time and also has a programme of temporary thematic exhibitions. The City of London began collecting works of art in the
seventeenth century, commissioning portraits of the judges who
assessed property claims in the wake of the Great Fire of
London of 1666. The collection now comprises 4,000 works of
art ranging from royal portraits to depictions of important sea
battles. Since the Second World War, it has concentrated on
London subjects. Among the most popular works in the
Guildhall collection are Dante Gabriel Rossetti's *La
Ghirlandata* and Millais' *The Woodman's Daughter* (his *Lorenzo
and Isabella* is also here). There is work by Landseer and James
Webb, Frederic Leighton's *The Music Lesson*, and a large landscape by John Constable, *Salisbury Cathedral from the Meadow*.
The Gallery also houses John Singleton Copley's famous (and
gigantic) *The Defeat of the Floating Batteries (Siege of Gibraltar)*.
Permanently on display is a selection from the hundreds of oils,
watercolours, and drawings by Matthew Smith bequeathed to
the gallery in 1974. In the basement is the remarkable site of

London's only Roman amphitheatre. Dating from the first century, it was designed to hold some 6,000 spectators and was discovered in 1988. The necessarily subdued lighting only heightens the impressive atmosphere.

Gunnersbury Park Museum

Gunnersbury Park, Pope's Lane, London W3 8LQ

020 8992 1612

www.hounslow.info/gunnersburyparkmuseum

Open: Daily, 11:00 AM–5:00 PM (–4:00 PM, Nov–Mar); closed 24–26 Dec.

Admission: Free

Underground: Acton Town

Gunnersbury Park Museum is the local history museum for the London Boroughs of Ealing and Hounslow, situated in the former nineteenth-century home of a branch of the Rothschild family in Gunnersbury Park. Opened in 1929, the museum has since collected a wide range of objects, paintings, and photographs that reflect life in the two boroughs from prehistory to the present day and still continues to gather material. The collections are now so large that most of them are in storage, but they are brought out for public view through a programme of regularly changing exhibitions, and items not on show can be viewed by appointment. Among the objects featured are a Stanhope printing press of 1804, a group of seventeenth-century Hounslow swords, two carriages from around 1800 previously owned by the Rothschild family, numerous local history commemorative vessels, and a large number of items of pharmaceutical glass and pottery donated by local pharmacists.

Handel House Museum

25 Brook Street, Mayfair, London W1K 4HB (entrance at back)
020 7495 1685
www.handelhouse.org

Open: Tu–W and F–Sa, 10:00 AM–6:00 PM; Th, 10:00 AM–8:00 PM;
Su, noon–6:00 PM. During recitals, the Rehearsal Room is closed;
please phone to check.
Admission: £5.00; Concessions, £4.50; Children, £2.00
Underground: Bond Street

The Handel House Museum opened to the public in 2001, after
several rooms had been restored to accord with their eighteenth-
century originals. The museum is located on the upper floors of
25 and 23 Brook Street, where George Frideric Handel lived
between 1723 and his death in 1759, writing some of his most celebrated music: the "Fireworks Music," "Zadok the Priest" (for
the coronation of George II), and, of course, "The Messiah"
(1741). The upper floors of 23 Brook Street, which have also
been restored, were home to the rock guitarist Jimi Hendrix for
a year and a half in 1968–1969; they now provide a space for
changing exhibitions and events, as well as for the Byrne collection of manuscripts, portraits, and printed scores. The museum
visit begins with a brief video introduction, followed by a tour of
the house, in the course of which the visitor is familiarized with
Handel's music, life, and times. There are displays of fine and
decorative arts, including musical manuscripts, early editions of
operas and oratorios, letters, prints, and portraits from the collection. Handel himself owned more than eighty paintings by the
time he died, and the museum displays works borrowed from
major collections as well as its own holdings.

HMS *Belfast*

Morgan's Lane, Tooley Street, London SE1 2JH
020 7940 6300
www.iwm.org.uk

Open: Daily, Mar–Oct, 10:00 AM–6:00 PM; Nov–Feb, 10:00 AM–5:00
PM (last admission 45 minutes before closing); closed 24–26 Dec.
Admission: £9.95; Concessions, £6.15; Children under 16, Free
Underground: London Bridge/Tower Hill

HMS *Belfast* was launched in March 1938 and commissioned
into the Royal Navy on 5 August 1939, just before the outbreak of the Second World War, in which she played an
important role. Closely involved in the Battle of the North
Cape, which resulted in the sinking of the *Scharnhorst*, *Belfast*
also supported the advancing Allied troops as they made their
way onto Gold and Juno beaches on the morning of D-Day, 6
June 1944, was one of the very first ships to open fire on
German positions in Normandy and remained almost continu-
ously in action for the next five weeks. The most considerable
surviving example of Britain's twentieth-century naval power,
Belfast was the first ship to be saved for the nation since
Nelson's HMS *Victory* and, since October 1971, has served as
a museum moored on the Thames between Tower and London
Bridge. There are nine decks in all, devoted to representations
of life on board during the Second World War, the conditions
in which up to 950 crew members lived and fought until the
Belfast's retirement in 1963, and the history of the Royal Navy.
Since becoming an Imperial War Museum site in 1978, *Belfast*
has registered over six million visitors.

Hogarth's House

Hogarth Lane, Great West Road, Chiswick, London W4 2QN
020 8994 6757
www.hounslow.info/hogarthshouse.htm

Open: Tu–F, 1:00 PM–5:00 PM (closes 4:00 PM in winter); Sa–Su,
1:00 PM–6:00 PM (closes 5:00 PM in winter)
Admission: Free
Underground: Turnham Green; 190 bus

The painter and engraver William Hogarth lived here during
the last fifteen years of his life. The house was then in the
country, a rural summer retreat (from his home and studio in
Leicester Square) on the edge of the old village of Chiswick,
but is now perilously near the rush and roar of traffic on the
Great West Road. The house was built around 1700 and has
survived, to a very large extent, as Hogarth would have known
it. Though damaged during the Second World War, it was
restored by the local council, and its gardens, behind high brick
walls, still contain a mulberry tree more than 300 years old.
Hogarth occupied the house with his wife, sister, and mother-
in-law; his wife lived on here after Hogarth's death until 1789.
It was first opened to the public in 1904 and contains the
largest collection of Hogarth's engravings permanently on display (others of his works crop up in several museums and historic houses around London). These include *Harlot's Progress*,
Rake's Progress, *Marriage à la Mode*, and also *Gin Lane* and *Beer
Street*, prints of both of which can be bought at the house,
together with books and postcards of Hogarth's works. His
tomb is in the graveyard of the nearby St. Nicholas' Church.

Horniman Museum

100 London Road, Forest Hill, London SE23 3PQ
020 8699 1872
www.horniman.ac.uk

Open: Daily, 10:30 AM–5:30 PM; closed 24–26 Dec.
Admission: Free
Train: Forest Hill (from London Bridge)

Frederick Horniman, one of two sons of the tea merchant John Horniman, began collecting articles on his travels in the 1860s, mainly in Africa and the Near East. An avid collector, he also procured many more items through the London auction houses and opened part of his home to the public so they could view the riches he had amassed. When the collections outgrew the available space, Horniman commissioned Charles Harrison Townsend to design a new museum. This opened in 1901, and Horniman then gave the building and its surrounding land to the people of London. He died in 1906. A new building was donated by Frederick's son Emslie in 1911, and a new extension was added in 1999 (a project completed in 2002).

The Horniman collections number some 350,000 items in three main areas: ethnography (world cultures); natural history, which includes 250,000 specimens; and a large collection of musical instruments. There are also educational, library, and archival collections. The museum maintains an active collecting policy with curators carrying out regular fieldwork to acquire new objects (and to find out more about existing ones). Over 90% of the collections of ethnography and music have been acquired since Frederick Horniman's original bequest. The

Horniman Natural History Collections cover the entire range of natural science areas, from butterflies and wasps to rocks and geological specimens. There is a revitalized aquarium; a hundred species of fish, amphibians, reptiles, and plants; and several interactive displays.

Music making around the world is represented by one of the most comprehensive collections of musical instruments in the UK. There are over 7,000 objects made to produce sound, and the collection embraces instruments of traditional and contemporary music drawn from dozens of countries, from zithers to bagpipes, from a Moroccan lute to Nigerian Ibo pot drums, from the variety artiste Joan Stonehewer's musical saw and sleigh bells to the classical Iranian dulcimer, flute, and spike fiddle. Among the outstanding examples of stringed instruments once owned by Arnold Dolmetsch is a German baroque lute, dating from the mid-eighteenth century. The oldest item here is a pair of bone clappers in the form of human hands, made in Egypt around 1500 BC, while electric guitars and synthesizers dating from the 1990s are among the most recent acquisitions. Recordings of dozens of instruments are also available to visitors.

But the backbone of the Horniman museum has always been ethnography. With its almost 80,000 objects, and particularly strong in its holdings of African culture, it is widely regarded as one of the most significant in the country, along with those of the Pitt-Rivers Museum in Oxford and, of course, the British Museum. There are also major American and Pacific collections, as well as an Asian collection comprising some 30,000 items, including doors and archways from India, puppets and masks from Nepal, Japan, Sri Lanka, and China. There are also exhibits of folk art from Scandinavia and other parts of Europe.

Hunterian Museum (Royal College of Surgeons)

Royal College of Surgeons, 35-43 Lincoln's Inn Fields, London WC2A 3PE

020 7869 6560

www.rcseng.ac.uk/museums

Open: Tu–Sa, 10:00 AM–5:00 PM

Admission: Free

Underground: Holborn

At the heart of the Hunterian Museum collection are more than 3,000 anatomical and biological specimens collected by the museum's founder, John Hunter (1728-1793), in association with his brother William. The strong narrative thread running through the collection is that of the development of surgical practice since the eighteenth century and the exploration of the interactions of art and science. On the upper floor, the Science of Surgery exhibition traces the increasing specialization of modern surgery. There is a detailed display of items from the Lister collection, illustrating his theories of antisepsis and anaesthetics.

Highlights include the Evelyn anatomical tables, bought in Italy by the diarist John Evelyn in 1646; the Minimal Access Training Unit, which allows visitors to test their aptitude for keyhole surgery; the skeleton of the celebrated Giant O'Brien; and George Stubbs' painting of a yak, which was brought back alive to England by Warren Hastings, the first British governor-general of India.

Imperial War Museum

Lambeth Road, London SE1 6HZ

020 7416 5000

www.iwm.org.uk

Open: Daily 10:00 AM–6:00 PM; closed 24–26 Dec.

Admission: Free

Underground: Lambeth North/Elephant & Castle

The Imperial War Museum has a vast and incomparable collection that covers all aspects of twentieth- and twenty-first-century conflicts involving Britain and the Commonwealth. The museum affords extensive access to its huge behind-the-scenes collections, which encompass a staggering wealth of material, including over 14,000 works of fine art, paintings, drawings, and sculptures and an unrivalled collection of some 30,000 international war posters; 120 million feet of cine film and at least 6,500 hours of videotape; 36,000 hours of interviews and recordings in the Sound Archive; and six million photographs, negatives, and transparencies. The Department of Printed Books contains over 100,000 volumes plus tens of thousands of pamphlets, periodicals, technical drawings, and maps. Of the ten permanent galleries, some cover the major twentieth-century conflicts and others are devoted to recurrent themes.

The Large Exhibits Gallery displays weapons and vehicles mainly from the two World Wars. The military section has tanks and howitzers, while the naval section has big guns, underwater craft, and the smallest surviving fishing craft to have taken part in the evacuation from Dunkirk in 1940, the

Tamzine. Among the air warfare exhibits are aircraft from both British and German services, a Sopwith Camel and a Zeppelin observation car from the First World War; a Spitfire and a Focke Wulf 190 from the Second. The extensive First World War Galleries are concerned with the continuing debate about the origins of the conflict; the Western Front and the appalling conditions in trench warfare; war in the air, at sea, and on other fronts; poets and painters; and the home front. One highlight is the walkthrough re-creation of a 1916 trench, with special effects of lighting and sounds — and smells.

The Holocaust Exhibition takes as its starting point the violently unstable political scene in Europe immediately after the First World War, looks at the Europe-wide phenomenon of anti-Semitism, and traces the rise of the Nazi party. Photographs, documents, newspapers, artefacts, posters, and film, as well as individual mementoes, diaries, and albums, offer stark evidence of persecution and slaughter, collaboration and resistance, and the resilience and luck that allowed some to survive. Art galleries on the second floor are devoted to paintings, drawings, and sculpture produced by artists who served in major conflicts. The John Singer Sargent Room houses Sargent's famous canvas, *Gassed* (1918), 20 feet by 9, a haunting image of men blinded by mustard gas, based on what the artist had seen in France in 1918.

There is a gallery honouring those awarded the George Cross and the Victoria Cross. There is also a permanent exhibition devoted to Field Marshal Montgomery, which was opened to coincide with the sixtieth anniversary of the Battle of El Alamein. Among the items on display are Montgomery's school reports; his orders, decorations, and medals (including the diamond-encrusted Order of Victory awarded to him by Stalin); and the surrender document signed by the Germans at Montgomery's headquarters in May 1945.

Another major part of the museum's displays focuses on the many conflicts since 1945. Crimes against Humanity, at the centre of which is a specially made thirty-minute film, explores genocide and ethnic violence and the elements in common with Nazism in campaigns of mass murder carried out in Armenia, East Timor, Rwanda, Bosnia, Cambodia, and elsewhere. The museum's holdings can be seen as a dreadful testament to the most destructive century the world has to show thus far — yet they also serve as a testament to extraordinary resilience, courage, loyalty, stoicism, and the fierce desire for self-determination, independence, and a peaceful and productive life.

Jewel Tower

New Palace Yard, Abingdon Street, London SW1P 3JX
020 7222 2219
www.english-heritage.org.uk/server/show/ConProperty.104

Open: 10:00 AM–5:00 PM (Apr–Oct), to 4:00 PM (Nov–Mar); closed
24–26 Dec and 1 Jan.
Admission: £2.90; Concessions, £2.20; Children, £1.50. May close for
special functions; please call to check before travelling.
Underground: Westminster

Built circa 1365, originally to house the treasures of Edward
III, the three-storey Jewel Tower, or King's Privy Wardrobe, is
one of only two buildings of the original Palace of
Westminster to survive the disastrous fire of 1834 (some of the
proposed designs for the rebuilding of the Houses of
Parliament are displayed here). Notable features include a fourteenth-century ribbed vault and the remnants of the moat and
the medieval quay outside. The permanent exhibition devoted
to the history and work of Parliament includes a touch-screen
computer on which the visitor can take a virtual tour of the
Commons and the Lords. The Westminster Sword, dating
back to around AD 800 and unearthed nearby in 1948, is on
display here, as are items of pottery retrieved from the moat.
The second floor now includes new illustrated panels, telling
the story of this small but important building that functioned
as the storehouse for official parliamentary documents, then as
the Board of Trade's Standards Department (weights and
measures) from 1869 until just prior to the Second World War.

Jewish Military Museum and Memorial Room

Shield House, Harmony Way (off Victoria Road), Hendon, London, NW4 2BX

020 8202 2323

www.ajex.org.uk/museum.htm

Open: M–Th, 10:30 AM–4:30 PM. Appointment necessary. Guided tours are available in the afternoons from 2:30 PM to 4:30 PM.
Admission: Free.
Underground: Hendon Central

Founded by the Association of Jewish Ex-Servicemen and Women, the museum commemorates in its displays the contribution to the Armed Forces of the Crown made by British Jews over the last two centuries, though, unsurprisingly, it concentrates on the two World Wars. Its memorial window was designed by Abram Games, one of the twentieth century's most influential graphic artists, who produced many official posters during the Second World War and designed the BBC logo. There are over 1,000 items on display, consisting of memorabilia, pictures, medals, uniforms, and letters, mostly donated by veterans and their families. The museum, as well as housing the Jewish book of Honour from the First World War, is currently engaged in compiling a Roll of Honour of the more than 60,000 Jewish personnel who served in the British forces between 1938 and 1960.

Jewish Museum, Camden

129-131 Albert Street, NW1 7NB
020 7284 1997
www.jewishmuseum.org.uk

Open: M–Th, 10:00 AM–4:00 PM; Su, 10:00 AM–5:00 PM; closed
Fridays, Saturdays, and Jewish and public holidays.
Admission: £3.50; Concessions, £2.50; Children and Students, £1.50
Underground: Camden Town

Founded in 1923, the Jewish Museum began in Woburn House
in Bloomsbury. It relocated to Camden Town in 1995 and
amalgamated, on a two-site basis, with the former London
Museum of Jewish Life (now the Jewish Museum, Finchley).
With the aid of panels, maps, and artefacts, three galleries trace
the thousand-year history of Jews in England, from the invita-
tion extended by William I, through their expulsion in the late
thirteenth century and eventual readmission by Oliver
Cromwell, up to the present. There is a small but interesting
collection of paintings, including portraits by Solomon Hart,
Thomas Hudson, and Tilly Kettle together with drawings and
historic prints from the Alfred Rubens collection. The
Photographic Archive consists primarily of black-and-white
photographs of Jewish life in London over the last century.
These include many images of weddings, holidays, and other
aspects of family life, as well as the world of work and Yiddish
theatre. Other photographs reflect the experiences of refugees
and the broader story of the Diaspora. The museum has an
internationally significant collection of Judaica, including marriage rings and Hanukah lamps, silver Torah ornaments, and a
seventeenth-century Venetian synagogue ark.

Jewish Museum, Finchley

Sternberg Centre, 80 East End Road, Finchley, London N3 2SY
020 8349 1143
www.jewishmuseum.org.uk
Open: M–Th, 10:30 AM–5:00 PM; Su, 10:30 AM–4:30 PM; closed
Fridays, Saturdays, Jewish and public holidays, and 24 Dec–4 Jan,
also Sundays in August and Bank Holiday weekends.
Admission: £2.00; Children 12 and under, Free
Underground: Finchley Central; twelve-minute walk via Station Road
and Manor View.
Buses: 82, 143, 326, 460

The Finchley site of the Jewish Museum is primarily educational, holding a wide range of social history material, including
everyday objects, photographs, documents, and oral history
interviews. This reflects the diverse roots and everyday life of
Jewish people, with particular strengths in the history of the
Jewish East End and Jewish immigration to this part of
London and settlement there. It also seeks to represent the
experiences of Jewish refugees and Holocaust survivors. There
is a Holocaust Education Gallery, which traces the story of
Leon Greenman, an Auschwitz survivor, born in England.

Keats House

Keats Grove, London NW3 2RR
020 7435 2062
www.cityoflondon.gov.uk/keats

Open: Tu–Sa, 10:00 AM–noon for schools and pre-booked visits; 1:00
PM–5:00 PM for all visitors; Su and Bank Holidays, 1:00 PM–5:00 PM
for all visitors; closed all Mondays except Bank Holidays. Note: Keats
House will close on 31 October 2007 for the final stage of its exten-
sive restoration and will re-open in late summer 2008.
Admission: £3.50; Concessions, £1.75; Children under 16, Free;
Garden, Free
Underground: Hampstead

Charles Wentworth Dilke and Charles Armitage Brown,
friends of Keats, originally built two semidetached houses: they
were converted into one by a later owner. Keats moved into
the house with Brown at the end of 1818, after the death of his
brother Tom, and stayed until the autumn of 1820. It is the setting that produced some of his most memorable poetry: "Eve
of St. Agnes," "La Belle Dame Sans Merci," and "Ode to a
Nightingale," which was written in the garden. During his
time here, Keats also fell in love with Fanny Brawne, whose
family moved into the other house of the pair in 1819, and it
was from this house that he travelled to Rome, where he died
of tuberculosis aged just 25. The museum opened in 1925 after a
public subscription raised sufficient money to preserve the
building, and it retains a number of original features. It also
contains a substantial collection of items related to Keats and
his circle: letters, manuscripts, paintings, books, and furniture.
There is a brooch made partly from Keats's hair and the
engagement ring that he offered Fanny Brawne.

Kensington Palace

Kensington Palace Gardens, W8 4PX
0870 751 5170
www.hrp.org.uk

Open: Mar–Oct, 10:00 AM–6:00 PM; Nov–Feb, 10:00 AM–5:00 PM
(last admission one hour earlier); closed 24–26 Dec.
Admission: £12.00; Concession, £10.00; Children under 16, £6.00;
Children under 5, Free
Underground: High Street Kensington/Queensway/Notting Hill Gate

Kensington Palace was once a favoured home of Britain's monarchs and the setting for many great events in royal history. Originally the Earl of Nottingham's private country house, the building was acquired by William III and Mary II in 1689 and adapted for royal residence by Sir Christopher Wren. The palace later played host to the courts of Queen Anne, George I, and George II. Queen Victoria was born and spent her childhood here and actually held her first Privy Council meeting here, on the day of her accession to the throne. More recently, the palace was home to Diana, Princess of Wales, who had apartments here from 1981 to her death in 1997; the palace then became the central point of extraordinary scenes of public mourning. The King's apartments are rather grander than the Queen's; and while the King's Gallery boasts work by Bassano and Tintoretto, the Queen's Gallery contains family portraits—but also a full-length depiction of Peter the Great painted by Sir Godfrey Kneller during the Tsar of Russia's 1698 visit. The Royal Ceremonial Dress Collection displays an exhibition of court dress from the eighteenth century to the present, which particularly features Princess Diana's dresses.

Kenwood House

Hampstead Lane, London NW3 7JR

020 8348 1286

www.english-heritage.org.uk

Open: Apr–Oct, 11:00 AM–5:00 PM; Nov–Mar 11:00 AM–4:00 PM; closed 24–26 Dec and 1 Jan.

Admission: Free

Train: Hampstead Heath, one and a half miles

Underground: Archway or Golders Green, then bus 210

This remarkable house, poised on the edge of Hampstead Heath, was remodelled by Robert Adam for Lord Mansfield between 1764 and 1779, by enlarging the building and enhancing existing rooms. The richly decorated library is widely regarded as one of Adam's great masterpieces. The first Earl of Iveagh bought Kenwood House in 1925. When he died two years later, he bequeathed the estate and part of his collection of pictures to the nation. The Iveagh bequest includes important works by Rembrandt, Constable, Vermeer, Turner, Reynolds, and Gainsborough. Constable's *Hampstead Heath with Pond and Bathers* now hangs, of course, close to the place where it was originally painted. The Suffolk Collection on the first floor includes notable Elizabethan and Stuart portraits by William Larkin, Van Dyck, and Lely. The surrounding parkland, influenced by the great English landscape gardener Humphry Repton, offers lakeside walks and meandering woodland paths. Most of the grounds are accessible by gravel path and grass.

Leighton House Museum

12 Holland Park Road, Kensington, London W14 8LZ
020 7602 3316
www.rbkc.gov.uk/leightonhousemuseum

Open: W–M, 11:00 AM–5:30 PM; closed 25–26 Dec and 1 Jan.
Admission: £3.00; Concessions, £1.00
Underground: High Street Kensington

Leighton House Museum is the former studio-house of the
great Victorian artist Frederic, Lord Leighton (1830–1896),
who was President of the Royal Academy. He spent many
years abroad, travelled widely in Europe and the Ottoman
Empire, and incorporated many things he had collected—and
the enthusiasms that had prompted him to acquire them—into
his new house. It was built in 1864, and Leighton embellished
and extended it for the next thirty years. The Arab Hall is
probably the most remarkable feature, with its fountain, golden
mosaic frieze, and extraordinary chandelier. The ground floor is
notable too for William De Morgan's startling peacock-blue
tiles. Amidst all the sumptuous interiors and striking designs,
the large and sometimes grandiose Victorian canvases by Frith,
John Everett Millais, Alma-Tadema, Edward Burne-Jones, and
George Frederick Watts—Leighton's contemporaries—there
are many works by Leighton himself, quintessentially Victorian,
yet one of the most attractive is his *Courtyard in Algiers*, small,
unpretentious, and possibly quite easily overlooked amidst the
grandeur.

Library and Museum of Freemasonry

Freemasons' Hall, 60 Great Queen Street, London WC2B 5AZ

020 7395 9257

www.freemasonry.london.museum

Open: M–F, 10:00 AM–5:00 PM; Guided tours available—these must be booked in advance for Saturdays (when a booking fee is payable).

Admission: Free

Underground: Holborn/Covent Garden

Located on the first floor of Freemasons' Hall, originally intended as a memorial to freemasons who died in the First World War, and the third hall to be built on the site, the museum is reached via the extensive reference library. It contains a large number of artefacts bequeathed by masons or associated with them, including such celebrated masons as Winston Churchill, Edward VII, and Lord Kitchener, as well as some intriguing prints, engravings, and photographs. There are collections of pottery and porcelain (Wedgwood, Doulton, Meissen), glassware, and Masonic jewellery, together with an extensive display of regalia (medals, aprons, and sashes).

Highlights include the huge Chinese export porcelain punch-bowl, the processional sword of the United Grand Lodge of England, and the Barraclough Masonic Clock.

Linley Sambourne House

18 Stafford Terrace, London W8 7BH
M to F, 020 7602 3316 ext 300, 11:00 AM to 5:30 PM; Sa and Su,
020 7938 1295
www.rbkc.gov.uk/linleysambournehouse

Open: Mar–Dec, Sa and Su, 10:00 AM–5:00 PM; by appointment for
groups
Admission: £6.00; Concessions, £4.00; Children under 18, £1.00
Underground: High Street Kensington

All visits to the house, preceded by a brief video introduction
and lasting approximately one and a half hours, are by guided
tour only with set tour times on Saturdays and Sundays (most
weekend tours are conducted by an actor in period costume)
and at other times by appointment only. Linley Sambourne
House, dating from around 1870, is a striking example of a late
Victorian townhouse. Home to the cartoonist Edward Linley
Sambourne and his family from 1874, it survives with almost all
of its furniture and fittings intact. On the death of
Sambourne's wife in 1914, their son Roy took over the house
and left it to his sister on his own death in 1946. The house
offers a fascinating insight into the cultural preferences of an
artistic, middle-class family of the time, with the striking
stained-glass windows in drawing room and morning room, the
extensive use of William Morris wallpapers, and evidence of
the strong Japanese cultural influence that was so widespread in
Europe in the late nineteenth century.

London Canal Museum

12-13 New Wharf Road, King's Cross, London N1 9RT

020 7713 0836

www.canalmuseum.org.uk

Open: Tu–Su and Bank Holidays, 10:00 AM–4:30 PM (last admission 3:45 PM); closed over Christmas, but check with museum for exact dates.

Admission: £3.00; Concessions, £2.00; Children 6–15, £1.50; Children 5 and under, Free

Underground: King's Cross

This is the only London museum devoted to inland waterways, housed in a former ice warehouse that was built around 1862–1863 for the famous ice-cream maker Carlo Gatti. The museum features the history of the ice trade and ice cream as well as that of the canals. The collections explore the origins and development of the canal boat in the late eighteenth and early nineteenth centuries, illustrating the conditions in which canal families lived, the decline of canal boats as working instruments, and their subsequent rise in popularity as central to the leisure industry. There are explanations of how canal locks work and how boat designs changed over two centuries, as well as a collection of original folk art as exemplified by canal boat decoration. Visitors can also learn about the cargoes carried in the trade's heyday and the horses they used.

London Fire Brigade Museum

94a Southwark Bridge Road, Bermondsey, London SE1 0EG
020 7587 2894
www.london-fire.gov.uk

Open: M–F by guided tour at 10:30 AM and 2:00 PM. All visits are by
guided tour and need to be booked in advance, as each visit is tailored
to the needs of visitors.
Admission: Adults £3.00; Children 7–14, £2.00; Children under 7,
Free; Concessions and groups, £2.00 per person; School groups, Free
Underground: Borough

The museum is located in the London Fire Brigade's own
Training Centre, a building dating back to 1820, thirteen years
before its founding. It began as the London Fire Engine
Establishment, formed by pooling the resources of nearly a
dozen individual insurance company brigades. The museum
contains a wealth of information about the development of
firefighting appliances and an extensive collection of early fire
engines. It also houses a great many artefacts and miscellaneous
exhibits illustrating the history of firefighting in London from
the Great Fire of London in 1666 to the present day, including
the brigade's efforts during the famous fire of 1834. There is,
unsurprisingly, a strong emphasis on the Second World War
when the fire services were so crucial to the defence of the city
in the Blitz.

London Sewing Machine Museum

308 Balham High Road, London SW17 7AA

020 8682 7916

www.wimsew.com/acatalog/wimsew_catalog_London_Sewing_Machine
_Museum_79.html

Open: First Sa of every month, 2:00 PM–5:00 PM

Admission: Free (persons over 16 only), but donations are welcomed to specified charities: The Royal National Lifeboat Institute and Leukaemia Research. Note: There are 40 steps to the upper floor, no lift available.

Underground: Tooting Bec

The London Sewing Machine Museum, dedicated to the accomplishments of the company's founder, Thomas Albert Rushton, contains a replica of Rushton's original shop in Merton Road as well as over 600 domestic and industrial machines dating from the 1850s through to the 1950s. The feature attraction is a Wheeler & Wilson type machine given as a wedding present to Queen Victoria's eldest daughter, Victoria Adelaide Mary Louisa (known as Vicky), born in 1840, who married Frederick, Crown Prince of Prussia, who became Kaiser Frederick III. Amongst the domestic items on display is the original Singer No 1, developed in 1855, the first sewing machine by Isaac Merritt Singer (1811–1875).

London Transport Museum

Covent Garden Piazza, London WC2E 7BB
020 7379 6344
www.ltmuseum.co.uk

Open: Currently closed; call for updated information
Admission: Call for information
Underground: Covent Garden

Beginning with a modest collection of buses, the museum's holdings increased substantially with the addition of examples of public transport such as the tram and underground railway systems, motor buses, and trolley buses, as well as a strong showing of transport posters, with examples from some well-known names. The heart of the exhibition is the collection of bright red double-decker buses, which became an iconic image of London, recognized all over the world. The museum was, quite specifically, devoted to the London Transport company, responsible for the city's public transport for over seventy years, but it is now owned by Transport for London (formed in 2000), which has a wider remit.

While there are provisions for open weekends at the time of writing, the public galleries are closed for extensive work and due to reopen in the autumn of 2007. There will be repairs made to the roof and general improvements made to the building. The intention is to widen the range of exhibits to include cycling, walking, taxicabs, and river traffic.

Lord's Tour and MCC Museum

Lord's Cricket Ground, St. John's Wood, London NW8 8QN
www.lords.org

Open: Tours daily, Apr–Sept at 10:00 AM, noon, and 2:00 PM;
Oct–Mar at 10:00 AM and 2:00 PM; visitors are advised to book
ahead. There are no tours on major match days.
Admission: £10.00; Concessions, £7.00; Children, £6.00
Underground: St. John's Wood

The guided tour of Lords, widely regarded as the home of
English cricket, takes in the famous Long Room in the members' pavilion, built in 1890; the Committee Room; and the
Real Tennis Court, dating from 1900. The MCC Museum
(Marylebone Cricket Club, which owns and maintains the
ground) describes the game's 400 years of history with the help
of paintings, memorabilia, and numerous photographs. Among
the historic artefacts is one of W. G. Grace's cricket bats and a
cap worn by the great Australian batsman Sir Don Bradman
during the famous 1930 tour.

Its most precious exhibit must be the tiny Ashes urn, recently
sent to Australia as part of an historic touring Ashes
Exhibition. The Ashes came into being in 1882 when, following England's defeat by Australia and the publication of a
mock obituary for English cricket, the bails were burned and
the ashes preserved in the urn. The museum also houses the
Wisden Trophy, which is regularly contested by England and
the West Indies.

Museum in Docklands

No 1 Warehouse, West India Quay, Hertsmere Road, London E14 4AL
0870 444 3857
www.museumindocklands.org.uk

Open: Daily, 10:00 AM–6:00 PM
Admission: £5.00; Concessions, £3.00; Children under 16, Students, Unwaged, and Disabled Carers, Free
Underground: Canary Wharf; Station (DLR) West Ferry/West India Quay

This Georgian warehouse, one of many then providing secure storage for all the goods imported from the West Indies, was one of the largest brick buildings in the world when constructed as part of the original dock development. For a hundred years, the sheds and warehouses here stored every conceivable commodity, from spices and drugs to coffee, furs, and feathers. Carefully restored, No 1 Warehouse retains much of the original timber and brick. The museum vividly examines some of the major commodities traded through London, by means of a tobacco-weighing station, a re-creation of a bottling vault, and exhibits detailing the tobacco, timber, grain, and sugar trades. The galleries show how the docklands region, as well as the River Thames as a whole, has been at the heart of centuries of social and economic change. There are numerous artefacts, engravings, paintings, testimonies, and photographs drawn from the collections of the Museum of London and the Port of London Authority. A spectacular feature of the gallery is a 1:50 scale model of Old London Bridge, the first stone structure over the Thames.

Museum of Brands, Packaging and Advertising

2 Colville Mews, Lonsdale Road, London W11 2AR
020 7908 0880
www.museumofbrands.com
Open: Tu–Sa, 10:00 AM–6:00 PM; Su, 11:00 AM–4:00 PM (last
admission one hour before closing); closed Mondays except Bank
Holidays.
Admission: £5.80; Concessions, £3.50; Children 7–16, £2.00;
Children under 7, Free
Underground: Notting Hill Gate

Opened in 2005, this is a collection of some 10,000 products
and promotional items from the gigantic collection of founder
Robert Opie, illuminating 200 years of consumer behaviour.
From toys and comics to fashion design and advertisements,
teas and tobacco, cordials, soaps, and condiments, these pack-
ets, tins, and boxes from the best-known manufacturers as well
as the obscure, vanished, and forgotten must compose one of
the most evocative and nostalgic forms of social history. The
exhibits also trace the development of advertising from
Edwardian times through two World Wars, the fifties and the
swinging sixties, to the present day. They explore the impacts
of new brands on our daily lives and, of course, revive our own
memories of once-familiar objects and images.

Museum of Garden History

Lambeth Palace Road, London SE1 7LB

020 7401 8865

www.museumgardenhistory.org

Open: Tu–Su, 10:30 AM–5:00 PM; closed over Christmas period.

Admission: £3.00; Concessions, £2.50 (charges voluntary)

Underground: Lambeth North/Westminster

The world's first museum devoted to garden history is located at the deconsecrated church of St Mary-at-Lambeth on the south bank of the Thames, and is a building of considerable historic significance. Adjoining it is a seventeenth-century-style knot garden, filled with plants authentic to the period, which commemorates two famous gardeners, John Tradescant and his son (also John). The first was gardener to Lord Salisbury at Hatfield House and later gardener to Charles I. Sent abroad, Tradescant returned with oleanders and figs. His son, another adventurous plant hunter, went to Virginia and brought back a tulip tree, Michaelmas daisy, and Virginia creeper. The Tradescant family collection formed the basis of the great Ashmolean Museum in Oxford, and its founder, Elias Ashmole, is buried here. Near the Tradescant tomb in the garden is that of Captain William Bligh of HMS *Bounty* fame (whose house, marked by the usual blue plaque, is a few minutes' walk away). The museum has a useful brief display of developments in garden history and a very informative exhibition of celebrated plant hunters, such as Ernest Wilson, who introduced over a thousand new plants to Britain. There is an extensive and fascinating collection of tools: a pair of eighteenth-century hand shears, a sixteenth-century earthenware

Tudor thumb pot, and a watering pot of the next century, soon to be superseded by metal watering cans.

There are several items once owned by famous gardeners: Gertrude Jekyll's potting shed desk (and some of her letters) and the tweed Trilby that served as Sir Frederick Gibberd's gardening hat. There is a set of pony boots (worn by ponies when pulling lawnmowers to prevent grass damage) from 1900, a 1920 bee skep (for carrying bees to temporary locations), and a diverting selection of garden gnomes. The museum also has a notable research library and a significant holding of prints, photographs, bills and receipts, brochures, and catalogues, which together make up an invaluable cache of social history related to the history of gardens and gardening. Even strangers to gardening history will be grateful to John and Rosemary Nicholson, who founded the museum in 1977 and also saved this fine building from demolition. There is a plaque commemorating the Nicholsons in the garden.

Museum of London

London Wall, London EC2Y 5HN

0870 444 3851

www.museumoflondon.org.uk

Open: M–Sa, 10:00 AM–5:50 PM; Su, noon–5:50 PM; closed 24–26 Dec and 1 Jan.

Admission: Free

Underground: Barbican/St. Paul's/Moorgate

Due to a major programme of developments, the construction of new exhibition spaces and new visitor facilities, the lower galleries of the museum are currently closed. Until the new galleries open in the autumn of 2009, the permanent exhibition will consist of these four: London before London, Roman London, Medieval London, and Tudor and Early Stuart London.

The permanent exhibition galleries explore the story of London from prehistoric times until 1665-66, the years of the Great Plague and the Great Fire. Before London, there were ancient forests drowned by the great river, hunters, temporary settlements. Vivid, video timelines speed through centuries, the shifting landscape, cities built and abandoned, settlements initiated and laid waste.The exhibitions pay constant and close attention to the central importance of the River Thames - the River Wall includes some 300 objects dredged up from the river, among them tools and weapons tens of thousands of years old. After Boudicca's rebellion and the burning of the city in AD 60, London was rebuilt as a planned Roman town. Forty years later, it had replaced Colchester as the capital of the province. Roman London was the largest city in Rome's Britannia and the museum has many artefacts from that time, pottery, tools, glass vessels, coins and sculpture, the fascinating marble sculptures from the Temple of Mithras and a remarkable lead ingot from the first century, weighing 80 kilograms and stamped with the emperor's name.

The Medieval Gallery ranges through the crowded period from Anglo-Saxon times to Viking raiders and the Norman Conquest, with a fine selection of medieval jewellery and costume. The Tudor and Early Stuart Galleries take the story of London on through the great age of Henry VIII and Elizabeth I. This was a major period of expansion and royal palace-building but also saw the dissolution of the monasteries. The galleries continue the story up to the English Civil War, the killing of an English King, plague and fire.

Exhibits include paintings, engravings, maps, sculptures, posters, costumes, tools and machinery. They range from dazzling mosaics to the remarkable Cheapside Hoard of gold and silver jewellery. There are also many accomplished reconstructions and replicas: tremendous models of Roman settlements, prison cells from Newgate and Wellclose Square, and a late Saxon house. There is a section of the original London wall suddenly there, visible through a display window. And there are short films devoted to the Black Death and to the Great Fire, which destroyed four-fifths of the city in just four days.

The museum holds internationally recognized collections in a number of areas, including its dress collection, ceramics and Elizabethan and Jacobean jewellery. There will be much that delights and absorbs the interest of any visitor but children in particular will certainly be enthralled by many of the displays here: the living maps and models, the videos and reconstructions and a hubbub of voices, celebrating figures both famous and obscure, often quite unknown, in fact, the citizens who make, and make sense of, this or any other city.

Museum of the Order of Saint John

St. John's Gate, St. John's Lane, Clerkenwell, London EC1M 4DA
020 7324 4070
www.sja.org.uk/history

Open: M–F, 9:00 AM–5:00 PM; Sa, 10:00 AM–4:00 PM; only groups
need to book in advance.
Admission: Free (except for tours Tu, F, Sa at 11:00 AM and 2:30 PM)
Underground: Farringdon

The Order of Saint John was founded at the very end of the
eleventh century when the Crusaders captured Jerusalem: the
Knights Hospitaller, along with the Knights Templar, were the
main defenders of the Holy Land until the final Muslim victory in 1291. Little remains of the Priory of the Knights of St.
John, precursors of St. John's Ambulance. Among the museum's exhibits are architectural fragments; seals and numismatics,
including an important collection of Crusader coins; arms and
armour, mainly European plate armour but with an example of
Turkish Ottoman mail; drug jars and other items from the
Hospitallers' pharmacy in Malta; and decorative arts reflecting
the tastes of the European aristocratic families who supported
or joined the order. The paintings include images of the patron
saint of the Order, St. John the Baptist, portraits of grand
masters, knights and clergy, and sea and landscapes depicting
naval battles and views of Malta. Some of the banners captured by Napoleon's forces when he conquered the island in
1798 are displayed here.

National Army Museum

Royal Hospital Road, London SW3 4HT
020 7730 0717
www.national-army-museum.ac.uk

Open: Daily, 10:00 AM–5:30 PM; closed 24–26 Dec, 1 Jan, Good
Friday, and May Day.
Admission: Free
Underground: Sloane Square

The National Army Museum's collections illustrate nearly 600
years of British military history. They include a huge array of
uniforms, as well as weapons used by British and
Commonwealth soldiers, from the age of the longbow to the
present day. There are extensive archives of printed papers,
which include a warrant to raise troops signed by King Charles
I on the outbreak of the English Civil War (1642–1651), and
the order that launched the Charge of the Light Brigade in
1854. The photographic collection comprises at least half a million images dating from the 1840s to the present day, and displays also incorporate paintings, prints, books, and journals.
There are in excess of 7,000 items of personal equipment,
including iconic objects such as Florence Nightingale's lamp
and Lord Raglan's Crimean telescope. The collection also
includes scientific tools, musical instruments, and several types
of armour and horse furniture. From the history of the
Redcoats up to the Napoleonic Wars, other sections cover the
army's role in those wars, the defence and extension of the
British Empire during its nineteenth-century heyday, the two
World Wars, and the army's role in more recent conflicts, from
Aden and Cyprus to the Falklands and Iraq.

National Gallery

Trafalgar Square, London WC2N 5DN
020 7747 2885
www.nationalgallery.org.uk

Open: Daily, 10:00 AM–6:00 PM (W until 9:00 PM)
Admission: Free
Underground: Charing Cross/Leicester Square

The National Gallery's permanent collection, one of the finest
in the world, spans the period from about 1250 to 1900 and
includes all the major European schools of painting. It attracts
between four and five million visitors every year. In April 1824,
the House of Commons agreed to pay £57,000 for the picture
collection of the banker John Julius Angerstein. Intended to
form the core of a new national collection for the education
and enjoyment of the whole population, the thirty-eight paintings were first displayed at Angerstein's own house in Pall
Mall, but public criticism of such inadequate accommodation
for them led to the construction of a purpose-built gallery. A
site in Trafalgar Square was chosen, as the crossroads of
London, where the collection would be accessible to the rich
people travelling from West London in their carriages and to
the poor coming on foot from the East End. The National
Gallery mosaics, in the vestibule of the main entrance, were
designed and made by the artist Boris Anrep (1885–1969), from
the mid-1920s to the 1950s, and one of the cycle's most striking
features is Anrep's use of contemporary figures such as Virginia
Woolf as Clio, the Muse of History, and Greta Garbo as
Melpomene, the Muse of Tragedy. Sir Winston Churchill is
shown as "Defiance," Dame Margot Fonteyn as

"Delectation," and Bertrand Russell as "Lucidity" in the "Modern Virtues." On the lawns outside the gallery are a sculpture of James II, in bronze, from the studio of Grinling Gibbons and a replica of the statue of George Washington by the French sculptor Jean-Antoine Houdon (who also produced busts of Benjamin Franklin, John Paul Jones, and Thomas Jefferson).

From the outset, the National Gallery has been committed to education, and students have always been admitted to the gallery to study the collection and to make copies of the pictures. The Sainsbury Wing, completed in 1991, houses the early Renaissance collection, both the Italian and the Northern Renaissance, with a fine selection of works from German and Netherlandish painters. The late fourteenth-century Wilton Diptych is displayed here, as are Uccello's *Battle of San Romano* and Van Eyck's *Arnolfini Marriage*. There are also major works by Crivelli and Mantegna, Antonello da Messina's *St. Jerome in his Study* and Piero della Francesca's *The Baptism of Christ*. Paintings from other periods, generally on Level Two, are displayed in the West Wing (1500–1600), the North Wing (1600–1700), and the East Wing (1700–1900). There are too many celebrated, even iconic, works to do more than gesture toward a tiny portion of them. Among the finest examples from the sixteenth century are Holbein's *The Ambassadors*, Bronzino's *Allegory of Venus and Cupid*, Titian's *Bacchus and Ariadne*, and Leonardo's *Virgin of the Rocks*. The seventeenth-century holdings are notable for, among much else, the wonderful collection of Dutch and Flemish paintings, beneficiaries of two major bequests in the nineteenth century, one of them from former Prime Minister Sir Robert Peel.

The National Gallery has two of the thirty extant works by Vermeer: *A Young Woman Standing at a Virginal* and *A Young Woman Seated at a Virginal*. There is also Pieter de Hooch's *Courtyard of a House in Delft*, Hobbema's *Avenue at Middelharnis*, and his *The Haarlem Lock, Amsterdam*. Gerrit Dou is represented by *A Poulterer's Shop* and two portraits. Room 23 is devoted to Rembrandt: the National Gallery has over two dozen paintings by him, including *Belshazzar's Feast* and two self-portraits, one of them the remarkable *Self-Portrait at the Age of 34*. The great Velasquez canvas, *The Rokeby Venus*, damaged by the Canadian suffragette Mary Richardson in the spring of 1914, is here; so too is the startling Caravaggio painting, *The Supper at Emmaus*.

In the East Wing, the 1700–1900 period has too many superb works to list, among them one version of Van Gogh's *Sunflowers* and his memorable *Van Gogh's Chair*, painted in Arles in 1888, when Van Gogh and Gauguin were working together. There is Ingres' fine *Madame Moitessier* and the truly iconic John Constable painting of *The Hay Wain*, together with one of the most celebrated works of Thomas Gainsborough, his double wedding portrait of *Mr. and Mrs. Andrews*. When the National Gallery, in conjunction with the popular BBC Radio 4 current affairs programme, *Today*, conducted a poll in which the British public voted for what they regarded as the greatest painting in Britain, the winner was J. M. W. Turner's *The Fighting Temeraire*. That painting is here, together with other notable Turners, including the stunning *Rain, Steam, and Speed—The Great Western Railway*. Other immediately recognizable images are George Stubbs' *Whistlejacket*, Renoir's *Les Parapluies*, Rousseau's *Tiger in a Tropical Storm*, and Seurat's *Bathers at Asnières*. The visitor to the National Gallery can—and does, and should—wander, become caught and held, intend to make for some definite location, be caught and held again, fail to remember that intended destination, and recognize that it doesn't matter. Ideally, make several visits, start each at different points—and let the pictures guide you.

National Maritime Museum

Romney Road, Greenwich, London SE10 9NF

020 8312 6565

www.nmm.ac.uk

Open: Sept–Jun, 10:00 AM–5:00 PM; Jul–Aug, 10:00 AM–6:00 PM
(last admission 30 minutes prior to closing); closed 24–26 Dec and on
the day of the annual London Marathon.

Admission: Free

Underground: Cutty Sark DLR

The National Maritime Museum's collection contains over
two million objects related to the story of Britain at sea: the
histories of the Royal and Merchant Navies, navigation,
astronomy, timekeeping, marine art, and much else. It was for-
mally established by act of Parliament in 1934 and opened to
the public by King George VI on 27 April 1937. It has benefited from some major bequests, particularly that of Sir James
Caird, which incorporated the huge collection of paintings,
drawings, and prints, the A. G. Macpherson collection, which
Caird had bought in the late 1920s.

The museum's British portraits collection is only exceeded in
size by the National Portrait Gallery, and its holdings related
to Nelson and Cook are unrivalled. It has the world's largest
maritime historical reference library, which includes books dating back to the fifteenth century. A new gallery, including
around 250 objects from the Museum's collections, is devoted
to Britain's Royal Navy in the late Georgian period and
Nelson's role in it, looking at the issues which contributed
towards the Navy's reputation and success and the different

experiences of officers and ordinary sailors at this turbulent time. Among the several major collections, one of the finest is that of marine art. It comprises around 4,500 oil paintings alone, ranging from sixteenth-century portraits by Peter Lely to Turner's *Battle of Trafalgar*, commissioned for George IV and the largest picture Turner ever produced. Twentieth-century artists represented here include Alfred Wallis, L. S. Lowry, and Edward Wadsworth. Other holdings include flags; uniforms; maps and manuscripts; weapons, from daggers to cannon; a major holding of over 3,000 ship models; and an internationally significant collection of timekeepers, among them several marine chronometers by John Harrison, who was finally recognized in 1773 as having solved the problem of longitude.

National Portrait Gallery

2 St. Martin's Place, London WC2H 0HE
020 7306 0055
www.npg.org.uk

Open: Sa–W, 10:00 AM–6:00 PM; Th–F, 10:00 AM–9:00 PM; closed
Good Friday, 24–26 Dec, and 1 Jan.
Admission: Free
Underground: Leicester Square/Charing Cross

The National Portrait Gallery presents a history of Britain
through paintings, photographs, sculptures, and drawings. Its
collection of more than 330,000 works finds room for painters,
poets, princes, criminals, queens, and philosophers, from the
later fourteenth century to the present. Founded in 1856, the
gallery opened three years later, and its original intention was to
display images of great Britons. Among the men responsible
for its foundation were Thomas Carlyle and Thomas
Macaulay, both biographers and historians with an intense
interest in their country's past. The criterion at the outset was
that the status of the subject was of primary importance, rather
than the quality of the image or the status of the artist. That
criterion is still used, but, notwithstanding, there are a great
many fine paintings and drawings. The gallery has been on its
present site, next to the National Gallery, since 1889.

In 1928, the eminent art dealer and benefactor Sir Joseph
Duveen agreed to fund a major extension, which was opened
by George V and Queen Mary in 1933. Another new wing
opened in 2000, dramatically expanding the space available. An
astoundingly successful exhibition in 1968 of photographs by

Cecil Beaton, attracting 75,000 visitors, followed by the opening of a new department devoted to photography and film, ensured that photography continues to maintain a major presence in the galleries.

The Ondaatje Wing houses the extraordinarily rich Tudor and Stuart Collection. Portraits are shown in broadly chronological order, beginning with a room devoted to the early Tudors and their predecessors. There is a striking portrait of Henry VII painted in 1505, the earliest painting in the collection, and Holbein's celebrated cartoon of Henry VII and Henry VIII. The Elizabethan paintings are set in a contemporary version of a Tudor long gallery, and include the gallery's first ever acquisition, a portrait of William Shakespeare, displayed here along with the "Ditchley" portrait (by Marcus Gheeraerts the Younger) of Elizabeth I. The extraordinary portrait of Edward VI in distorted perspective is accompanied by a new, specially designed viewing device, enabling National Portrait Gallery visitors to see the painting in correct perspective for the first time.

A room housing the collection of early portrait miniatures completes the suite of Tudor Galleries and includes Nicholas Hilliard's earliest portrait of Elizabeth I, painted in 1572, showing the queen bedecked with jewels and flowers, as well as portraits of her courtiers and favourites, including Sir Francis Drake and Walter Ralegh. The redesigned seventeenth- and eighteenth-century galleries provide improved access to some of the country's finest portraits, including those of Charles I, Nell Gwyn, Samuel Pepys, and Bonnie Prince Charlie. The newly refurbished Regency displays feature naval and military heroes (Nelson, Wellington) and eminent writers (Austen,

Wordsworth). In other rooms, aristocrats and celebrities are balanced by tributes to such engineering heroes as Brunel and Stephenson.

The newly re-hung Balcony Gallery display concentrates on Britain between 1960 and 1990, what are sometimes termed the "Pendulum Years" and a period marked by extraordinary social and political changes, not least in Britain's altered status on the world stage. There was a ten-year rule in operation (the period that must elapse after a subject's death before an image could be displayed in the gallery), but that was relaxed in 1969, and now there are representations, frequently photographic, of numerous celebrated contemporary figures.

Natural History Museum

Cromwell Road, London SW7 5BD

020 7942 5000

www.nhm.ac.uk

Open: M–Sa, 10:00 AM–5:50 PM; Su, 11:00 AM–5:50 PM (last
admission 5:30 PM); closed 24–26 Dec.

Admission: Free

Underground: South Kensington

The Natural History Museum first opened its doors to the
public on Easter Monday in 1881, but its origins go back more
than 250 years. The major initial impetus came from physician
and collector of natural curiosities, Sir Hans Sloane, who left
his immense collection of more than 70,000 items to the
nation in 1753. Sloane's specimens originally formed part of the
British Museum, but as other collections were added, including specimens collected by botanist Joseph Banks on his
1768–1771 voyage with Captain James Cook aboard HMS
Endeavour, it became increasingly obvious that the natural history elements would need their own home. Sir Richard Owen,
Superintendent of the British Museum's natural history collection, persuaded the government that a new museum was
required. The chosen architect, Captain Francis Fowke, died
suddenly in 1865, and the contract was awarded instead to a rising young architect from Manchester, Alfred Waterhouse.
Waterhouse altered Fowke's design from Renaissance to
German Romanesque, creating the beautiful Waterhouse
Building. By 1883, the mineralogy and natural history collections were in their new home, but the collections were not
finally declared a museum in their own right until 1963.

With more than 70 million specimens, the museum is home to the largest and most important natural history collection in the world. The scope of its specimens is simply vast: they include material from the ill-fated dodo to meteorites from Mars. They cover almost all groups of animals, plants, minerals, and fossils, and range in size from cells on slides to whole animals preserved in alcohol. In total, there are fifty-five million animals, including twenty-eight million insects, nine million fossils, six million plant specimens, more than 500,000 rocks and minerals, and 3,200 meteorites in the collections. The library holds the largest collection of natural history library materials in the world, including books, periodicals, original drawings, paintings and prints, manuscripts, and maps.

The museum's main division is between the Life Galleries and the Earth Galleries. The Central Hall is dominated by the skeleton of a Diplodocus, while in small alcoves leading off the Hall, some remarkable items can be found: a coleocanth fossil, a jade boulder weighing more than 500 kilograms, a tangle of interlocking gypsum crystals. Above the Hall, at its far end, is a trunk section of a giant sequoia, more than thirteen hundred years old when it was felled in 1892. The Life Galleries, part of the original Natural History Museum, house some of the earliest displays, an outstanding collection of minerals and another of birds, in splendid Victorian cabinets, and include the extinct Mauritius dodo. The dinosaurs include a Triceratops skeleton and an animatronic Tyrannosaurus Rex. Other galleries focus on human biology, mammals (the world's diversity demonstrated by fossil examples of extinct mammals alongside examples of their living relations and an astounding life-size model of a Blue Whale dwarfing the other specimens), and fossils. The Darwin Centre recently closed to visitors during a period of development (though there is still access to the centre by means of tours only: call 0207 942 5011).

The Earth Galleries (the Exhibition Road entrance) begin with Visions of Earth, an extraordinary avenue of sculptures, leading to an escalator that rises up through a gigantic model of the Earth. Other galleries demonstrate the treasures of the earth, minerals, gemstones, and rocks; and the power within it, the explosive force unleashed by volcanoes and earthquakes (there is an earthquake simulator), as well as, more broadly, the ways in which natural forces constantly shape and reshape the landscape of the planet. From the Beginning traces the story of evolution of life on earth and demonstrates the late stage at which human beings appeared on the planet. Next to the West lawn of the museum, the Wildlife Garden contains thousands of plant and animal species, from marsh marigolds to pheasant. With other displays devoted to primates and creepy-crawlies, this is the ideal destination for inquisitive children — but adults find plenty to amaze and stimulate them too.

North Woolwich Old Station Museum

Pier Road, North Woolwich, London E16 2JJ

020 7474 7244

www.newham.gov.uk/Services/MuseumsAndGalleries/

Open: Sa–Su, 1:00 PM–5:00 PM, Jan–Nov; during school holidays, the museum is open every afternoon, 1:00 PM–5:00 PM

Admission: Free

Train: North Woolwich; D. L. R.: King George V

Bus: 473, 474

The North Woolwich Old Station Museum, housed in a restored mid-Victorian station building, is devoted to the golden age of the railway. The exhibits include engines, carriages, models and furniture, posters, timetables, and other memorabilia, and there is a reconstruction of a 1920s ticket office. A miniature railway runs on the first two weekends of the month in the afternoon, with a charge for rides. There are also Steam Days, usually on the first Sunday of each month, when the working locomotives steam up and down outside. It is best to telephone to confirm times. There is an exhibition about the railways of East London and their impact on the areas they served and lots of hands-on activities for children.

Old Operating Theatre Museum and Herb Garret

9a St. Thomas Street, London SE1 9RY

020 7955 4791/ 020 7188 2679

www.thegarret.org.uk

Open: Daily 10:30 AM–5:00 PM; closed 15 Dec–5 Jan.

Admission: £5.25; Concessions, £4.25; Children under 16, £3.00

Underground: London Bridge

This is the oldest operating theatre in London and, reached by a steep, winding stair, is located in the roof space of what was, until the mid-nineteenth century, the parish church of St. Thomas's Hospital. It was rediscovered in 1956, restored and opened as a museum in 1962. The theatre is small but would have served as an ideal teaching area for the students who attended operations as spectators after the Apothecary's Act of 1815, which made it compulsory for apprentice apothecaries to gain practical experience. The garret was used by the apothecary to store and cure his herbs after the church was rebuilt in the early eighteenth century. Less vulnerable to rats than a basement, the garret was also preferable because its massive timbers stabilise the environment and absorb excess moisture. During restoration, several poppies were found in the rafters. Poppies are used to prepare opium, which was a very important and widely used medicinal plant. Other displays here deal with the history of surgery and the discovery of antisepsis by Lister.

Old Royal Naval College

Greenwich Hospital, King William Walk, London SE10 9LW

020 8269 4747

www.oldroyalnavalcollege.org

Open: The Painted Hall and the Chapel, daily, 10:00 AM–5:00 PM
(please check before making special trip); Grounds are open 8:00
AM–6:00 PM; closed 24–26 Dec.

Admission: Free

Underground: Jubilee Line to Canary Wharf and change to Docklands
Light Railway

The Old Royal Naval College is set in the centre of the
Maritime Greenwich World Heritage Site. Greenwich
Hospital was established in 1694 by Royal Charter for the relief
and support of seamen and their dependants and for the
improvement of navigation. Sir Christopher Wren planned the
site, and during the first half of the eighteenth century, various
illustrious architects, including Nicholas Hawksmoor and Sir
John Vanbrugh, completed Wren's grand design. The elaborate
ceiling and wall paintings in the Great Hall, part of the King
William Court, were executed by Sir James Thornhill between
1707 and 1726: the Painted Hall has been termed the finest dining hall in the Western World, and figures represented in the
hall include Isaac Newton, Copernicus, and John Flamsteed,
the first Astronomer Royal. The Painted Hall stood empty
until January 1806, when the body of Admiral Lord Nelson
was brought here to lie in state after the Battle of Trafalgar.
The chapel has been restored almost to its 1789 state. In 1869,
the hospital was closed; and in 1873, the complex of buildings
became the Royal Naval College, where officers from all over

the world came to train in the naval sciences. The Navy moved out in 1998 to a new Joint Services Staff College in Shrivenham.

Percival David Foundation of Chinese Art

53 Gordon Square, London WC1H 0PD
020 7387 3909
www.pdfmuseum.org.uk

Open: M–F, 10:00 AM–12:30 PM and 1:30 PM–5:00 PM; closed public holidays.
Admission: Free
Underground: Russell Square/Euston Square/Goodge Street

Scholar and collector Sir Percival David presented to the University of London in 1950 both a library of books relating to Chinese art and culture and the extensive collection of Chinese ceramics now housed in the museum. Concentrating on the period between the tenth and eighteenth centuries, the museum contains around seventeen hundred pieces, a number of which have previously been in Chinese imperial collections. There are many examples of stoneware from the Song (960–1279) and Yuan (1279–1368) dynasties, blue and white temple vases with fourteenth-century inscriptions, and a number of fifteenth century doucai wares.

Highlights include the model of a (rather grumpy) hare: T'ang dynasty, fifteen hundred years old; a table screen, with underglaze blue decoration, containing in its central panel a quotation (in Arabic) from the Koran: Ming dynasty, Zhenngde mark and period (1506–1521); and white porcelain figures of the twin spirits of harmony and happiness.

Petrie Museum of Egyptian Archaeology

University College London, Malet Place, London WC1E 6BT

020 7679 2884

www.petrie.ucl.ac.uk

Open: Tu–F, 1:00 PM–5:00 PM; Sa, 10:00 AM–1:00 PM (Tu and W mornings are devoted to visits by school parties)

Admission: Free

Underground: Goodge Street

The Petrie Museum is one of the most significant collections of Egyptian and Sudanese archaeology in the world, with an estimated 80,000 objects. It was founded in 1892 by the writer and traveller Amelia Edwards but is named after the initial occupant of what was the first UK chair in Egyptology, Sir Flinders Petrie. The collection was hugely augmented by Petrie's own excavations in Palestine and Egypt. The extensive holdings of everyday objects, from tools and weapons to amulets and jewellery, provide a unique insight into how people have lived and died in the Nile Valley. Exhibits include one of the earliest pieces of linen from Egypt (about 5000 BC), two lions from the temple of Min at Koptos (about 3000 BC), and the earliest examples of both metal and glazing from Egypt. The museum also houses the world's largest collection of Roman period mummy portraits (first to second centuries AD).

While the university has plans to re-house the Petrie Museum in purpose-built galleries on three floors of a new building, the Panopticon, this is not expected to open until 2008.

Pitzhanger Manor

Walpole Park, Mattock Lane, Ealing, London W5 5EQ
020 8567 1227
www.ealing.gov.uk/services/leisure/museums_and_galleries

Open: Tu–F, 1:00 PM–5:00 PM; Sa, 11:00 AM–5:00 PM
Admission: Free
Underground: Ealing Broadway

Sir John Soane, the English architect best remembered for designing the Bank of England, bought Pitzhanger Manor in 1800 and demolished the original house to create the villa. It became his own country residence, but he sold the property in 1810, and for most of the nineteenth century it was the home of the five daughters of Spencer Perceval, the Tory Prime Minister assassinated in the lobby of the House of Commons in 1812. After 1985 the Borough of Ealing restored the property and transformed it into a museum. Soane created intimate domestic interiors, decorated in neo-classical style, echoing his town house in Lincoln's Inn Fields. The Monk's Dining Room in the basement of the Soane block once held some of the architect's collections of architectural fragments and sculpture. The Victorian wing of Pitzhanger Manor now houses an impressive collection of Martinware, the highly decorated pottery produced between 1873 and 1923 and very fashionable in the late-Victorian period. Much of the original landscaping, which was carried out in 1800 by John Haverfield of Kew for Soane, has been retained. Although the lake is now a sunken garden, the bridge constructed by Soane can be seen, and his gateway and lodge have survived.

Prince Henry's Room

17 Fleet Street, London EC4Y 1AA

020 7936 2710

www.cityoflondon.gov.uk/Corporation/leisure_heritage/architectural_heritage

Open: M–Sa, 11:00 AM–2:00 PM

Admission: Free

Underground: Blackfriars/Temple/Chancery Lane

This is one of the few houses in London that predates the Great Fire of London in 1666. The history of the site can be traced back to the twelfth century when it formed part of the property granted to the Knights Templar, which, in 1312, passed to the Knights Hospitallers of the Order of St. John of Jerusalem. In 1610 the owner of the property decided to rebuild. The new building became a tavern, known for the next thirty years as the Prince's Arms. The Prince in question was the elder son of King James I, and this room served as the office from which he administered the Duchy of Cornwall. Henry died of typhoid in 1612, aged only eighteen. Prince Henry's Room, with its ornate plasterwork and fine wood panelling contains a small exhibition devoted to the great diarist Samuel Pepys. Whilst working as Secretary to the Admiralty, Pepys chronicled the Great Plague in 1665 and was surely the most famous witness to the Great Fire of 1666.

At the time of writing, the house is closed to the public pending future refurbishment, but it is expected to reopen during late 2007.

Queen's Gallery

Buckingham Palace Road, London SW1A 1AA
020 7766 7301
www.royal.gov.uk

Open: 10:00 AM–5:30 PM (last admission 4:30 PM)
Admission: £8.00; Concessions, £7.00; Children under 17, £4.00;
Children under 5, Free
Underground: Victoria/Green Park

The Queen's Gallery is located at Buckingham Palace but has
its own entrance. The original building was designed by John
Nash and completed in 1831, converted into a private chapel for
Queen Victoria in 1843 but destroyed in an air raid in 1940.
The Queen's Gallery was built in 1962 but was recently (and
very extensively) enlarged. The changing exhibitions in the permanent display space draw from the huge royal collection, one
of the world's finest. Its history extends back to Henry VIII,
while many of the acquisitions can be dated to the reign of
Charles I, a remarkable collector. Charles purchased—or was
presented with—numerous works by such painters as Titian,
Mantegna, Raphael, Rubens, and van Dyck, who was
employed as the King's principal painter. The holdings include
what is widely regarded to be one of the world's best collections of seventeenth-century Dutch pictures, notably
Vermeer's *A Lady at the Virginals with a Gentleman*, together
with exceptional works by such old masters as Leonardo da
Vinci, Canaletto, Lorenzo Lotto, Holbein, and Dürer.
Exhibits, which extend far beyond painting, include remarkable
examples of furniture, jewellery, porcelain and sculpture, manuscripts, and decorative arts objects by Fabergé and many others.

Queen's House

Romney Road, Greenwich, London SE10 9NF
020 8312 6565
www.nmm.ac.uk

Open: 10:00 AM–5:00 PM (last admission 4:30 PM); closed 24–26
Dec; also closes early some Fridays and Saturdays for special events:
please telephone to check.
Admission: Free
Underground: Cutty Sark DLR

The Queen's House was intended for James I's wife, Anne of
Denmark, according to tradition, to serve as an apology to Anne.
The King had sworn at her in public, after she accidentally shot
one of his favourite dogs while hunting in 1614. In 1616 Anne
commissioned Inigo Jones (1573–1652), who had risen to fame as a
designer of court entertainments and was appointed Surveyor of
the King's Works in the following year, to design a new pavilion
for her at Greenwich (there is a portrait of Jones by William
Dobson here). It was Jones's first major commission, principally
modelled on a Medici family villa. Anne died, however, during
the course of its construction, and by the time it was finally completed in 1637, Charles I had given Greenwich to his queen,
Henrietta Maria. It served various Royal residential purposes
thereafter. After a 2001 refurbishment, the building is now able to
show the National Maritime Museum's art collection, including
work by Reynolds, Hogarth, and Gainsborough; royal portraits;
and notable seascapes. Among the survivals from the original
building are the ironwork of what were termed the "tulip stairs,"
actually the first centrally unsupported spiral stair in Britain, and
the hall's remarkable marble floor, laid in 1635.

Ragged School Museum

46-50 Copperfield Road, London E3 4RR

020 8980 6405

www.raggedschoolmuseum.org.uk

Open: W, Th, 10:00 PM–5:00 PM; first Su of each month, 2:00 PM–5:00 PM

Admission: Free

Underground: Mile End; Limehouse (DLR)

The Ragged School Museum opened in 1990 in three canalside warehouses saved from demolition by a local campaign. It sets out to chart the history of the East End of London, and particularly the Copperfield Road Ragged School. Originally built in 1872, the buildings were taken over by Dr. Thomas John Barnardo to house his ragged school. By 1896, over a thousand boys and girls, aged between five and ten, received their breakfast and dinner here as well as a free education. After they were closed down by London County Council as unfit for education, the buildings were put to various uses until the formation of the Ragged School Museum Trust which now runs the museum.

There is a large and constantly increasing collection of objects associated not only with the history of ragged schools but, more broadly, with local history, industry, and life in the East End. Upstairs, a re-created classroom of the late nineteenth-century period gives visitors a vivid sense of how the Victorian poor were taught.

Ranger's House

Chesterfield Walk, Blackheath, London SE10 8QX
020 8853 0035
www.english-heritage.org.uk/server/show/conProperty.110

Open: end Mar–end Sept, M–W, Su, 10:00 AM–5:00 PM; Oct–Mar,
pre-booked tours only; closed 22 Dec–28 Feb; please phone the
house for additional opening times: 020 8853 0035.
Admission: £5.50; Concessions, £4.10; Children, £2.80
Train: Greenwich or Blackheath from Charing Cross or London Bridge

Ranger's House was built in the early eighteenth century, and
the broad avenue running up to it is part of the design by
Andre le Nôtre, who laid out the Versailles gardens. In the
mid-eighteenth century, it was the home of the Earl of
Chesterfield and became the official residence of the "Ranger
of Greenwich Park" after 1815, when the post was held by
Princess Sophia Matilda, niece of George III. It now houses
the Wernher Collection of paintings, porcelain, bronzes, and
one of the finest collections of Renaissance jewellery in Britain.
The diamond magnate Sir Julius Wernher (1850–1912) was a
tireless and discriminating collector, with a particular liking for
Fabergé. The nearly 700 works of art include Gabriel Metsu's
Interior with Lady Seated at the Keyboard and works by Hans
Memling, Joos van Cleeve, and Sir Joshua Reynolds. There is
a fine collection of porcelain, especially Sèvres, tapestries,
enamels, and silverware.

Royal Academy of Arts

Burlington House, Piccadilly, London W1J 0BD
020 7300 8000
www.royalacademy.org.uk

Open: Sa–Th, 10:00 AM–6:00 PM; F, 10:00 AM–10:00 PM; closed
24–25 Dec.
Admission: charge
Underground: Piccadilly Circus/Green Park/Oxford Circus/Bond Street

The Royal Academy was founded in 1768 with Sir Joshua
Reynolds as its first president. It has held a summer exhibition
every year since then, as well as staging highly prestigious international loan exhibitions. The permanent collection (not all on
display at any one time) comprises one work by each current
and former academician and focuses on British art and artists.
Many exhibits are "diploma works," presented to the academy
by the artist on the occasion of his or her election to member-
ship. Turner's 1800 *Dulbadern Castle* is a celebrated example of
such works, but there are also paintings by Constable, Sargent,
Millais, Fuseli, Hockney, and Spencer and sculpture by
Flaxman, Palaozzi, and Frink. The academy has also benefited
from many gifts and bequests. The collection now contains
about 850 paintings, 350 sculptures, 500 plaster casts, 15,000
prints and drawings, and 2,000 historic photographs. The academy has had its moments of drama: the Suffragette attack on
Sargent's portrait of Henry James in 1914, for instance, and the
extraordinary crowds eager to see David Wilkie's *Chelsea
Pensioners Reading the Gazette after the Battle of Waterloo* in 1822
and W. P. Frith's *Derby Day* in 1858, which necessitated the
roping off of the paintings for their protection.

Royal Academy of Music Museum

1 York Gate, Marylebone Road, London NW1 5HT
020 7873 7373
www.ram.ac.uk/museum

Open: M–F, 11:30 PM–5:30 PM; Sa–Su, noon–4:00 PM
Admission: Free
Underground: Baker Street/Regents Park

The permanent exhibitions at the Royal Academy of Music York Gate Collections are each displayed on a different floor of the building and are drawn from the academy's extensive holdings of instruments, pictures, and documents from the 1820s to the present. The Treasures of the Academy display includes original scores from Liszt and Brahms and items from the private collection of Sir Henry Wood, including his stopwatch. The String Gallery on the first floor has instruments by Stradivari, Amati, and Rugeri, alongside portraits of influential performers and composers. There is a display devoted to the making of stringed instruments, and resident luthier David Rattray can be seen maintaining the academy's stringed instrument collection. The Piano Gallery features pianos from the private collection of Kenneth and Mary Mobbs, generously loaned by them to the Royal Academy.

Royal Air Force Museum

Grahame Park Way, Hendon, London NW9 5LL

020 8205 2266

www.rafmuseum.org.uk/london/index.cfm

Open: Daily, 10:00 AM–6:00 PM; closed 24–26 Dec and 1 Jan and 8–12 Jan.

Admission: Free. Children under 16 must be accompanied by an adult at all times. Unfortunately advance notice of closures cannot be given: please telephone to check.

Underground: Colindale. Museum is a seven-minute walk from the station on the Edgware branch of the Northern Line. Please alight at Colindale, not Hendon Central.

Bus: Route 303 passes the museum entrance.

Britain's only national museum dedicated to aviation displays over 100 full-sized aircraft, in five hangars, from its total collection of well over 200. The aerodrome and training school were set up at Hendon in 1909, the year after Louis Blériot's flight across the English Channel, and the site was later used for the great air shows that took place between the wars. The displays outline the history of aviation, from the first balloon flights and the early wooden biplanes, through such famous war planes as the Battle of Britain Spitfires and Lancaster Bombers of the Second World War, through to the latest jet fighters and other military aircraft. Other exhibits include service vehicles, among them the Ford Model T tender and the Daimler Ferret armoured car; paintings, drawings, posters, and photographs, including the extensive collection of the aviation photographer Charles Brown; and medals, uniforms, aero engines, and weapons.

Royal College of Music Museum of Musical Instruments

Prince Consort Road, Knightsbridge, South Kensington, London SW7 2BS

020 7591 4842

www.rcm.ac.uk

Open: Tu–F, 2:00 PM–4:30 PM during term time or by appointment

Admission: Free

Underground: South Kensington

The Royal College of Music's Museum of Instruments houses an internationally renowned collection of over 800 instruments and accessories from circa 1480 to the present (700 European, keyboard, stringed, and wind; 100 Asian and African). A number of generous gifts and bequests since the foundation of the college in 1883 have hugely augmented its holdings, and in 1970, the collection was rehoused in a new museum. Highlights of the current collection include one of the earliest surviving examples of both harpsichords and virginals, trombones once owned by Gustav Holst and Sir Edward Elgar, and a clavichord once owned by Joseph Haydn. There is also an example of the type of glass harmonica that Benjamin Franklin invented. Selections from the extensive holdings of portraits are displayed in the museum: they include Burne-Jones's portrait of Paderewski and a bust of Ralph Vaughan Williams by Jacob Epstein.

Royal College of Physicians

Heritage Centre, 11 St. Andrew's Place, London NW1 4LE
020 7935 1174
www.rcplondon.ac.uk/heritage

Open: M–F, 9:00 AM–5:00 PM for historical tours of the collections
and college building by appointment only
Admission: charge
Underground: Regent's Park/Warren Street/Great Portland Street

The Royal College of Physicians is the oldest medical institution in England, and its collections relate to the history of the
college and of the physician's profession. They range from portraits of Fellows since 1518 to Cecil Symons' extensive collection of medical instruments, which is on permanent display in
the college. Other exhibits include a magnificent William IV
ear trumpet, tongue scrapers, nipple shields, medicine spoons,
and feeding cups. Among other notable items are William
Harvey's demonstration rod and the college's silver-gilt mace,
which dates from 1683 and shares its design with the House of
Commons mace. There is also the celebrated silver fluted
"Prujean" fruit dish, engraved with the coats of arms of Sir
Francis Prujean and his second wife Dame Margaret Fleming.
The dish may have been a wedding gift, as Sir Francis and
Margaret were married in Westminster Abbey in 1664. The
library has over 50,000 books and pamphlets of historical inter-
est, including sets of old journals and complete sets of *The
Lancet* and *British Medical Journal*.

Royal Fusiliers Museum

Tower of London, London EC3N 4AB
020 7488 5610

Open: M–Sa, 9:30 AM–5:30 PM; Su, 10:30 AM–4:30 PM (summer);
M–Sa, 9:30 AM–4:30 PM; Su, 10:30 AM–4:30 PM (winter); closed 25
Dec and 1 Jan.
Admission: Visitors pay the full entry fee for Tower of London and an
additional charge for this museum.
Underground: Tower Hill

The Royal Fusiliers Museum, which opened in 1962, is inside the Tower of London, the regiment's traditional home. The Fusiliers were formed in 1685 when Lord Dartmouth created the regiment from the Tower Guard, and this small museum tells the history of each of the regiment's campaigns, from its earliest battle for William of Orange against the French up to the present day. Recently, the regiment has been on peacekeeping duties in Northern Ireland and the Balkans. There is a display of paintings, uniforms, and medals highlighting the regiment's proud record of having had twenty of their members awarded the Victoria Cross, as well as a remarkable miniature display of the Peninsular War.

Royal Hospital Chelsea Museum

Royal Hospital Road, London SW3 4SR

020 7730 0161

www.chelsea-pensioners.co.uk

Open: M–Sa, 10:00 AM–noon and 2:00 PM–4:00 PM; Su, 2:00
PM–4:00 PM; closed Sundays, Oct–Mar, public holidays, and functions
(please check first).

Admission: Free

Underground: Sloane Square

The Royal Hospital, Chelsea, was designed by Christopher
Wren for Charles II when Chelsea was still a village some distance from London. It was founded for the benefit of invalided
or aged soldiers and around 400 retired soldiers still live there.
A statue of Charles II stands on the terrace. This small museum, originally opened in the Great Hall in 1866, explains the
history of the Chelsea pensioners. Its entrance hall is dedicated
to the memory of the Duke of Wellington, and there is a full-
length portrait of him by John Simpson, as well as George
Jones' panorama of the *Battle of Waterloo* (1820) and a diorama
depicting the Royal Hospital in about 1742. It is not possible to
visit the Long Wards, but there is a reconstruction of a typical
berth. Also on display is the uniform of a veteran soldier and
the collection of medals bequeathed by pensioners to the Royal
Hospital, which now number well over 2,000.

Royal London Hospital Museum

The Royal London Hospital, St. Augustine with St. Philip's Church, Newark Street, Whitechapel, London E1 2AA

020 7377 7608

www.bartsandthelondon.nhs.uk/aboutus/museums_and_archives.asp

Open: M–F, 10:00 AM–4:30 PM; closed Christmas, New Year, Easter, and public holidays.

Admission: Free

Underground: Whitechapel

Located in the former crypt of an extensively restored late nineteenth-century church, which also accommodates the Library of the School of Medicine and Dentistry at Whitechapel, the museum has a permanent exhibition of artefacts and archives relating to the hospital and the history of healthcare in the East End. Works of art, surgical instruments, medical and nursing equipment, uniforms, medals, and books are included. The museum is divided into three sections, covering the eighteenth, nineteenth and twentieth centuries. The displays feature such famous stories as those of nurse Edith Cavell, Joseph Merrick (the Elephant Man), a new section on forensic medicine (sponsored by crime writer Patricia Cornwell), which features original material on the Whitechapel (Jack the Ripper), Dr. Crippen, and Christie murders. There are also special sections on hospital uniform and on dentistry, including a denture made for George Washington.

Royal Mews

Buckingham Palace Road, London SW1
020 7766 7302
www.royalcollection.org.uk

Open: Daily except F, 11:00 AM–4:00 PM, 24 Mar–27 Jul and 26
Sept–31 Oct; daily except F, 10:00 AM–5:00 PM, 28 Jul–25 Sept.
Closed during State visits. Please phone to check.
Admission: £7.00; Concessions, £6.00; Children under 17, £4.50;
Children under 5, Free
Underground: Victoria/Green Park

The Royal Mews is a working stable, which has been in its
present location since 1760, and houses the State vehicles, both
horse-drawn carriages and motor cars, used for coronations,
State visits, Royal weddings, the State Opening of Parliament,
and other official engagements. Visitors can see the Gold State
Coach that was last used during the Golden Jubilee celebrations in 2002 to carry the Queen and Prince Philip to the
Service of Thanksgiving at St. Paul's Cathedral. It was built, at
a cost of some £8,000, for George III in 1762. For most of the
year, the stables are home to the working horses that play an
important role in the Queen's official and ceremonial duties.
They are mainly Cleveland Bays, the only British breed of carriage horse, and the Windsor greys, which by tradition always
draw the carriage in which the Queen is travelling. As they
may be on duty, undergoing training, or having a well-deserved
rest away from London, the horses are not always on view.

Royal Observatory, Greenwich

Greenwich Park, London SE10 9NF

020 8312 6535

www.rog.nmm.ac.uk

🏛 🎥 🖼 ⚒

Open: Daily, 10:00 AM–5:00 PM (last admission 4:30 PM); closed
24–26 Dec.

Admission: Free

Underground: Maze Hill/Greenwich

The Royal Observatory, now part of the National Maritime
Museum, is home to the Prime Meridian line and to
Greenwich Mean Time, which has been the official basis of
time management since 1884. Founded by Charles II in 1675, it
was the official government observatory from then until 1948.
Charles appointed John Flamsteed as the first Astronomer
Royal, and Flamsteed House was built by Sir Christopher
Wren in 1675–1676. When the lights of London became too
bright, the astronomers moved to Sussex, while the
Astronomer Royal is now based at Cambridge. The official
starting point for each new day, year, and millennium (at the
stroke of midnight GMT as measured from the Prime
Meridian), the Royal Observatory now houses displays of
astronomical instruments, clocks, and chronometers. Its Time
and Space project will include a new state-of-the-art planetari-
um, new galleries exploring astronomy and time, an education
centre, and an horology workshop. Visitors to the observatory
can stand in both the eastern and western hemispheres simulta-
neously by placing their feet on either side of the Prime
Meridian — the centre of world time and space.

Royal Pharmaceutical Society

1 Lambeth High Street, London SE1 7JN

020 7572 2210

www.rpsgb.org/informationresources/museum

Open: M–F, 9:00 AM–5:00 PM (limited areas). There are further displays on the first floor, and these can be viewed as part of a guided tour. The tours take place on Tuesdays at 2:00 PM and 4:00 PM, and places may be booked by telephone. There is level access to all parts of the museum displays.

Admission: Free

Underground: Lambeth North/Vauxhall/Waterloo/Westminster

The society has had a museum since 1842, which began as a collection of materia medica, with both authentic and adulterated samples of drugs and other substances, for teaching purposes as well as for research. Augmented by a number of large donations during the nineteenth century, much of the collection is now included in the Economic Botany Collection at the Royal Botanic Gardens, Kew. The items on display here include traditional dispensing equipment; drug storage containers, including fine Lambeth delftware from the seventeenth and eighteenth centuries; proprietary medicines; mortars; caricatures and photographs; and spoons, syringes, display glassware, and other practical accessories.

Royal Society of Arts

8 John Adam Street, London WC2N 6EZ

www.rsa.org.uk

020 7930 5115

Open: First Su of every month (except Jan), 10:00 AM–1:00 PM; otherwise open by appointment.

Admission: Free

Underground: Charing Cross

The Society for the Encouragement of Arts, Manufactures and Commerce first met in Covent Garden in 1754 and its first medals were awarded in 1756. Early members included Benjamin Franklin, William Hogarth, and Samuel Johnson. It held London's first exhibition of the works of living artists in 1760 and, after a period in temporary premises, moved in 1774 to premises in the Adelphi (just behind the Strand), especially designed for it by Robert Adam, its Great Room decorated with allegorical paintings (1777–1801) by James Barry, where it remains. Barry's series of six paintings — The progress of human knowledge and culture — has been described by critic Andrew Graham-Dixon as "Britain's late, great answer to the Sistine Chapel." The large collection of paintings held on loan from the Arts Council Collection by the RSA includes works by Frank Auerbach, Elizabeth Frink, and Lucien Freud.

Saatchi Gallery

www.saatchi-gallery.co.uk/

Charles Saatchi has been one of Britain's most influential and controversial collectors and exhibitors of contemporary art in recent years. Now the Saatchi Gallery is moving to Chelsea and will open in its new premises in November 2007. The Duke of York's HQ, Sloane Square, offers an impressive environment in which to view contemporary art, with very large well-proportioned rooms and high ceilings. The gallery will occupy the entire 50,000-square-foot building, giving the gallery scope for a book shop, educational facilities, and a café/bar. The Triumph of Painting exhibition will be on hold until the new gallery opens.

Saint Bartholomew's Hospital Museum

North Wing, Saint Bartholomew's Hospital, West Smithfield, London
EC1A 7BE

020 7601 8152

www.bartsandthelondon.nhs.uk/aboutus/st_bartholomews_hospital.asp

Open: Tu–F, 10:00 AM–4:00 PM; closed Christmas, New Year, Easter,
and public holidays. Checking by telephone advised before making a
visit.

Admission: Free, but donations welcome.

Underground: St. Paul's/Barbican

The museum tells the story of this famous institution and
explains its place in history. Videos, sound recordings, and life-
size models combine to illustrate and illuminate the hospital's
past. Among the exhibits, and one of the most important
treasures of the hospital, is the agreement between Henry VIII
and the City of London, which re-founded the hospital, a
magnificent document, complete with Henry's Great Seal.
Also on display are works of art, surgical and medical equipment, amputation instruments, and the tools of the apothecary's trade, including pill-making equipment, scales, and drug
bottles. Visitors can learn about William Harvey, physician to
Barts from 1609–1643 and discoverer of the circulation of the
blood. The patients' diet in earlier times is explained, and a
volume of nineteenth-century drawings and watercolours illustrates particular diseases and cases in graphic detail. Equipment
used by nurses in their work is exhibited, such as feeding cups,
a hypodermic syringe, and items of uniform. Attention is also
paid to the hospital's role in the training of medical students.

Science Museum

Exhibition Road, South Kensington, London SW7 2DD
020 7942 4000
www.sciencemuseum.org.uk

Open: Daily, 10:00 AM–6:00 PM; closed 24–26 Dec.
Admission: Free
Underground: South Kensington

The Science Museum originated in the Great Exhibition of 1851, when Britain was at the height of imperial confidence, the workshop of the world as well as its financial powerhouse. In 1852, the Museum of Manufactures opened in Marlborough House, serving as a long-term display area for selected items from the Great Exhibition, and in 1853, Prince Albert, a great supporter of British science who had largely planned and managed the exhibition, outlined a general plan for the buildings to be erected on a newly purchased site at Kensington (out of the profits of the Great Exhibition), including Museums or Schools of Science and Industry.

Today, the Science Museum's huge collections are spread over seven floors, its more than three dozen galleries include some 2,000 hands-on exhibits, an accurate indication in itself of a crucial part of the museum's purpose: to educate and excite the young, particularly, to awaken and stimulate an active interest in science and its applications in everyday life. With total holdings of over 300,000 items, the museum continues to acquire and display objects representative of their disciplines and of the development of western science, technology, and medicine from around 1700 to the present day, concentrating on the historical conditions that produce such objects as much as on the objects themselves. In the basement are several hands-on galleries: the Launch Pad and the Secret Life of the Home and the Garden, providing firsthand demonstrations of science and technology, from kaleidoscopes and fibre optics to household gadgets.

The Ground Floor features the Story of Steam, over 300 years, in the Energy Hall, a display including many early engines; Space, telling the story of space exploration, and Making the Modern World. This major exhibition, ranging from around 1750 to the end of the twentieth century, uses 150 of the most significant objects from the museum's holdings, from Stephenson's 1829 "Rocket" and the Lumière Ciné-Camera and Projector to the Command Module from Apollo 10 and the first prototype of the Clock of the Long Now (designed to keep accurate time for 10,000 years), set in their historical contexts. On the first floor, in addition to displays devoted to time and weather (with fascinating collections of sundials and water clocks on the one hand and barometers on the other), there is Who Am I?, which considers recent advances in genetics and psychology in relation to the question of our similarities and differences when compared with other people and other animals.

The Second Floor includes displays devoted to the history of computing and to ships (incorporating several intriguing models and smaller displays such as Diving, Docks, and Marine Engineering). Among the Third Floor features are the eighteenth-century science gallery, containing impressive and often beautiful items of scientific apparatus collected by George III; and a major display detailing the history of flight that features such historically significant aircraft as the first British jet and the 1928 *Gipsy Moth* in which Amy Johnson became the first woman to fly solo from England to Australia, together with such iconic objects as a section of fuselage from the Blériot XI monoplane.

A major recent addition to the museum has been the Wellcome Wing, which extends over four floors, from the 450-seat IMAX cinema and the motion stimulator to the virtual world of Digitopolis. The top two floors of the museum offer Glimpses of Medical History, reconstructions of scenes from the Neolithic Age to the late twentieth century, an exhibition devoted to veterinary history, and the important Science and Art of Medicine, some 5,000 items used to illustrate the worldwide history of medicine.

Shakespeare's Globe

21 New Globe Walk, Bankside, London SE1 9DT
020 7902 1400
www.shakespeares-globe.org

Open: 9:00 AM–5:00 PM, May–Sept; 10:00 AM–5:00 PM, Oct–Apr
Admission: £9.00; Concessions for Students, Seniors, and Children
5–15
Underground: Southwark/London Bridge/St. Paul's/Mansion House

Open all year round, Shakespeare's Globe Exhibition is the
world's largest exhibition devoted to Shakespeare and
Shakespearean London. A combination of interactive displays
and practical demonstrations explores and illuminates many
aspects of Elizabethan theatre, including the design, making,
and fitting of actors' costumes; musical instruments; and special
effects (gore, storms, and spirits). Visitors can watch a sword-
fighting display, see a working printing press in action, and dis-
cover how actors are dressed in Elizabethan clothing. They can
even try on the armour in the Elizabethan tiring room. The
exhibition also explores the story of American actor and direc-
tor Sam Wanamaker's long struggle to rebuild the Globe as
close to the original site as possible and illuminates some of the
techniques employed in the reconstruction.

Sherlock Holmes Museum

221b Baker Street, London NW1 6XE
020 7935 8866
www.sherlock-holmes.co.uk
Open: Daily, 9:30 AM–6:00 PM except Christmas Day
Admission: £6.00; Children under 16, £4.00
Underground: Baker Street

This early nineteenth-century house has been designed as a facsimile of the rooms occupied by Sherlock Holmes and his companion and chronicler, Doctor Watson, in accordance with Sir Arthur Conan Doyle's descriptions in the four novels and fifty-six short stories. From the shop on the ground floor, selling deerstalker hats, books, and assorted Holmesian memorabilia, stairs lead up to the living rooms and bedrooms. Visitors are greeted by Mrs. Hudson, the housekeeper, or by one of the principals. In Holmes's study, objects familiar from the stories are in evidence: deerstalker, violin, Persian slipper, and chemical paraphernalia. A series of curious waxwork tableaux illustrate dramatic incidents or moments in the stories, and there is an extensive collection of Victorian miscellanea, contemporary books and magazines, and household items — and a collection of letters from Sherlock Holmes admirers around the world, some clearly written tongue-in-cheek, others, as clearly, not.

Sir John Soane's Museum

13 Lincoln's Inn Fields, London WC2A 3BP
020 7405 2107; 020 7440 4263 for group bookings
www.soane.org

Open: Tu–Sa, 10:00 AM–5:00 PM (6:00 PM–9:00 PM first Tu of each
month, by candlelight, tickets £5.00); closed Sundays, Mondays, Bank
Holidays, and Christmas Eve.
Admission: Free. Museum tour every Saturday at 11:00 AM, tickets
£5.00, limited in number. Groups (of more than 6 people) are regret-
tably excluded on Saturdays.
Underground: Holborn

Four years before his death in 1837, by means of an act of
Parliament, the architect Sir John Soane established his house
as a museum open to the public, while also stipulating that it be
kept, as near as possible, in the state in which it was left at his
death. Following a recent five-year restoration programme, the
house — actually three houses in what is a notably attractive
square — is now almost exactly as it was in 1837. Every room is
itself a work of art, with many cunning effects. There are art-
fully positioned mirrors, which both expand the apparent space
and create the illusion of further rooms

The massed ranks of antiquities range from tiny plaster busts to
the huge sarcophagus of Pharaoh Sethi I, which Soane bought
in 1824 after the British Museum had balked at the asking price
of £2,000. There is also a cast of the Apollo Belvedere, which
was previously at Chiswick House, in the possession of Lord
Burlington. And everywhere there is abundant evidence of a
tireless collector, a seemingly infinite number of alcoves, recesses,

nooks, and crannies in which a bronze, a scarab, a seal, or a plaster bust stand. The collections include oils, watercolours, or drawings by Turner, Reynolds, and Fuseli; and there are three Canaletto views of Venice, including the much-admired *Riva degli Schiavoni*. There are thousands of architectural drawings by Soane himself and by many others, including Robert Adam, Piranesi, and Christopher Wren.

There is also an extensive collection of sculpture, including dozens of pieces by John Flaxman, a friend of Soane, who executed a pencil sketch of Soane's wife. The visitor's eye is constantly caught, diverted, and surprised in this extraordinary building, which is even a valuable repository of miscellaneous materials, such as nails, screws, sash cords, bolts, and window latches. There is Sir Thomas Lawrence's portrait of Soane; Soane's study, packed with fragments of marble; Sir Robert Walpole's desk; Chinese tiles, porcelain, and a scroll (1721); and the Naseby jewel, a tiepin circa 1630, said to have been dropped by Charles I at the Battle of Naseby. Other highlights include Hogarth's two series—*A Rake's Progress* and *An Election*—and the breakfast parlour.

Somerset House

Strand, London WC2R 0RN
020 7845 4600
www.somerset-house.org.uk
Courtauld Institute 020 7848 2526
www.courtauld.ac.uk/gallery/index.html
Gilbert Collection 020 7240 9400
www.gilbert-collection.org.uk
Hermitage Rooms 020 7413 3398
www.hermitagerooms.com

Open: 10:00 AM–6:00 PM (last admission to galleries 5:15 PM);
closed 24–26 Dec and 1 Jan.
Admission: £5.00 to each gallery; Concessions, £4.00; Students,
Children under 18, and unwaged, Free; Joint-collection ticket (any two
galleries), £8.00; Three-day pass (all three galleries) also available,
£12.00
Underground: Temple/Covent Garden/Charing Cross/Embankment

The Courtauld Institute of Art Gallery has one of the most
important collections in Britain. It includes world-famous Old
Masters, but its unique strength lies in the richness of its
Impressionist and Postimpressionist paintings, together with an
outstanding prints and drawings collection, featuring works by
Michelangelo, Rembrandt, Cézanne, and Turner. The collection consists of around 530 paintings, 7,000 drawings and 15,000
prints as well as significant holdings of medieval, Renaissance,
and modern sculpture, ceramics, metalwork, furniture, and textiles. These have derived substantially from the bequest of private collections, and the works are shown in that way.

The Thomas Gambier Parry (1816–1888) Gallery, strong in early Florentine Renaissance painting, also extends to glassware, ivories, and metalwork. The Samuel Courtauld (1876–1947) Galleries reflect his extraordinary collection of Impressionist and Postimpressionist paintings, and include several of the best-known works of the late nineteenth century: Manet's *A Bar at the Folies-Bergère*, Renoir's *La Loge*, and Cézanne's *The Montagne Saint-Victoire*. Viscount Lee of Fareham (1868–1947), co-founder of the Courtauld Institute, also made a huge contribution to the institute's holdings in Italian Renaissance and, particularly, British eighteenth-century painting. The Princes Gate Bequest is named for the London address of Count Antoine Seilern (1901–1978), whose strong and enduring interest in Rubens resulted in a fine collection of both paintings and drawings by that artist, but also drawings by Rembrandt and Tiepolo and work by Oskar Kokoschka.

Galleries IX–XIV are devoted to the twentieth century. They include a substantial number of outstanding works on long-term loan from private collections and the Roger Fry (1866–1934) bequest, which featured works by Fry himself and his Bloomsbury colleagues Vanessa Bell and Duncan Grant. It also includes a number of significant Postimpressionist works, unsurprisingly, since Fry was instrumental in introducing Postimpressionism to Britain through the exhibitions he organized in 1910 and 1912 and through his championing of Paul Cézanne. The twentieth-century galleries have some superb works by Fauvist painters, by Braque, August Macke, and Wassily Kandinsky, as well as sculptures by Rodin and Archipenko.

The Gilbert Collection was formed over some forty years by the late Sir Arthur Gilbert and includes over 200 gold boxes, the majority of them snuff boxes, set with precious stones, some of them extraordinarily costly and intricate, masterpieces of the art. A number of the boxes were made for kings and emperors and they include six jewelled boxes of outstanding quality made for Frederick the Great of Prussia. Other major features of the collection are the portrait miniatures and Roman enamel mosaics, Italian mosaics, and an important collection of more than 300 pieces of silver and silver-gilt work, particularly French, German and Italian.

The Hermitage Rooms on the ground floor of the South Building of Somerset House seek to recreate, in miniature, the splendour of the Winter Palace and its various wings, which now make up The State Hermitage Museum in St. Petersburg. This imperial setting provides the backdrop for rotating exhibitions from the holdings of the State Hermitage Museum, now more than three million items, which include remarkable collections of Old Masters, Impressionist, and Postimpressionist paintings, as well as antiquities and items of Oriental art.

South London Art Gallery

65 Peckham Road, London SE5 8UH
020 7703 6120
www.southlondongallery.org

Open: Tu–Su, noon–6:00 PM
Admission: Free
Underground: Elephant & Castle then bus 171, 12; Victoria or Oval
then bus 36, 436 toward Lewisham/New Cross
Bus: 12 from Trafalgar Square; 36 or 436 from Victoria; 171 from
Waterloo Road

In 1868, the South London Working Men's College opened at 91 Blackfriars Road, marking the beginnings of what is now known as the South London Gallery (SLG). The principal was Professor T. H. Huxley (biologist, "Darwin's bulldog," and grandfather of Aldous Huxley); the manager was William Rossiter. The gallery opened on the present site in 1891, with the support of leading artists Edward Burne-Jones, G. F. Watts, and Sir Frederic Leighton, President of the Royal Academy. The permanent collection is based around a number of paintings donated by such prominent Victorian figures as Leighton, Ford Madox Brown, Millais, and Ruskin. It later began to build a collection of twentieth-century paintings, then a collection of prints, which includes work by Graham Sutherland, Patrick Heron, and John Piper. Exhibitions concentrate mainly on contemporary art, but works in the permanent collection, if not on display, can be seen by appointment.

Southside House

3-4 Woodhayes Road, Wimbledon Common, London SW19 4RJ
020 8946 7643
www.southsidehouse.com

Open: 60-minute guided tours at 2:00 PM, 3:00 PM, and 4:00 PM,
from Easter to end Sept on W, Sa, Su, and Bank Holidays. Closed during Wimbledon Tennis Fortnight. Please phone ahead to check if house
is open.
Admission: £5.00; Concessions, £4.00; Children, £2.50
Underground: Wimbledon; bus 93

Southside House was renovated by Robert Pennington in the
late seventeenth century and was restored after the Second
World War, though it has been maintained with little substantial alteration. Pennington's descendants still live here, and the
remarkable collections of furniture, paintings, and items of
strong historical interest reflect the centuries of unbroken own-
ership. There are several works by Van Dyck; one of George
Romney's portraits of Nelson's mistress, Emma Hamilton; and
the pearl necklace worn by Marie Antoinette on the day of her
execution. Hilda Pennington Mellor married Axel Munthe,
Swedish author of the bestselling *The Story of San Michele*, in
1910. It was Hilda and her youngest son, Malcolm, who
became responsible for the preservation of Southside. Hilda
also developed the gardens with an artful use of water and hid-
den pathways.

Spencer House

27 St. James's Place, London SW1A 1NR
020 7499 8620
www.spencerhouse.co.uk

Open: Su (except Jan and Aug) for guided tours only, lasting approximately one hour, every twenty minutes, starting at 10:45 AM; last tour at 4:45 PM
Admission: £9.00; Concessions, £7.00
Underground: Green Park

Spencer House was built in 1756–1766 for John, first Earl Spencer (an ancestor of Diana, Princess of Wales), and was one of the pioneer examples of neo-classical architecture. Following the death of the earl in 1783, the house was partly remodelled by the architect Henry Holland, who added the Greek Ionic columns in the Dining Room and the large mahogany doors in the Staircase Hall, the Ante Room, and the Library. The Spencer family continued to live at the house until 1895 when the building was let to a series of tenants; in 1926, it was substantially restored. During the Second World War, the house was occupied by the nation's nursing services. In 1985, it was bought by Lord Rothschild's bank, which has completed extensive renovation, bringing the house back as far as possible to its late eighteenth-century condition. The Dining Room ceiling was designed by John Vardy, after Inigo Jones' ceiling in the Banqueting House, Whitehall, and was restored after suffering bomb damage during the Second World War. Upstairs, the famous Painted Room was designed by James "Athenian" Stuart and largely completed by 1765. Among several notable works of art here are paintings by Joshua Reynolds, George Romney, and Benjamin West.

Spitalfields Centre Museum of Immigration & Diversity

19 Princelet Street, London E1 6QH

020 7247 5352

www.19princeletstreet.org.uk

Open: Some days and by appointment; phone to check. The house is rarely open to the public (perhaps a dozen or so days a year) because the building is too fragile.

Admission: Free, but donations urgently needed.

Underground: Shoreditch/Liverpool Street

Built in 1719, 19 Princelet Street became the home of Huguenot refugees who had fled religious persecution in France and later prospered along with many others in the silk weaving trade. Characteristic of many merchants' homes in Spitalfields of the time, the garret windows were enlarged to let in more light by which journeyman weavers might work. Later occupants of the house followed other professions as the domestic silk trade foundered. During the waves of immigration that followed the Irish famine and the pogroms of Eastern Europe, a group of Jewish emigrants, mostly from Poland, took a lease on the house and, in 1869, erected a synagogue, built out on the ground floor, extending over the garden, with a gallery for women and children. More recently, the story of the mysterious last tenant, David Rodinsky, was told in the justly celebrated book by Rachel Lichtenstein and Iain Sinclair, *Rodinsky's Room* (1999). A campaign has been launched to save this remarkable, unrestored house and to mount a permanent exhibition devoted to the history of the immigrants who have had such a formative influence on both London's East End and the country as a whole.

St. Bride's Crypt Museum

St. Bride's Church, Fleet Street, London EC4Y 8AM

020 7427 0133

www.stbrides.com

Open: M–F, 9:00 AM–6:00 PM; Sa, 11:00 AM–3:00 PM

Admission: Free

Underground: Blackfriars

For 500 years, Fleet Street has been the generic term for the Press, since Wynkyn de Worde, former apprentice to William Caxton, brought England's first printing press with moveable type alongside St. Bride's Church, near to the literate churchmen who would be his best customers. The printer Edward Winslow was married here in 1594 and became one of the leading Pilgrim Fathers as well as three-time Governor of Plymouth, Massachusetts. The great free-standing canopied oak reredos, crafted when St. Bride's was restored after the Second World War bombs, is a memorial to Winslow and the Pilgrim Fathers. One of the many churches destroyed in the Great Fire of London, St. Bride's was rebuilt to Sir Christopher Wren's design. In 1764, when lightning damaged the steeple and a Royal Society committee was appointed to decide upon the best method of safeguarding buildings, George III insisted that lightning rods with blunt knobs were better than the pointed ones invented by Benjamin Franklin, since Franklin was seen as the wicked spokesman of disaffected American colonists. The display in the crypt tells the story of the church and its curious archaeological treasures and also illustrates the story of the printing industry. There is a section of Roman pavement, revealed during the postwar repairs.

The Stephens Collection

Avenue House, East End Road, Finchley, London N3 3QE

020 8346 7812

www.london-northwest.com/sites/Stephens

Open: Tu–Th, 2:00 PM–4:30 PM

Admission: Free

Underground: Finchley Central

Dr. Henry Stephens, a classmate of John Keats at Guy's Hospital, was the inventor (in 1832) of the famous "Blue-Black Writing Fluid," later developed into ink. A family firm set up to manufacture it laid the foundations of a considerable fortune and Stephens' son, Henry Charles Stephens, enhanced the business substantially. He became an MP and devoted himself to a number of local issues, and the name of "Inky" Stephens has remained familiar to several generations of Finchley residents. In 1874, he bought Avenue House, adding a laboratory in which he conducted his experiments, and when he died in 1918, he left it to the people of Finchley. It opened to the public ten years later. The small museum here illustrates the history of the company and of the development of writing materials, the story of the Stephens family, and the story of Avenue House. The land on which the house stands was owned by the Knights Hospitallers from 1312 until it was seized by Henry VIII in 1540. The grounds were landscaped by Robert Marnock, and many rare trees were planted, most of which survive to this day. The house was restored following a fire in 1989.

Sutton House

2 & 4 Homerton High Street, Hackney, London E9 6QJ
020 8986 2264
www.nationaltrust.org.uk

Open: Th–Su, 12:30 PM–4:30 PM, 1 Feb–23 Dec and Bank Holidays
Admission: £2.70; Children, 60p; Family, £6.00
Underground: Hackney Central (Silverlink from Highbury & Islington)

A fascinating survival in London's East End and the oldest domestic house in the area, Sutton House was built in 1535 by Sir Ralph Sadleir, secretary to Thomas Cromwell, rising star at the court of Henry VIII and eventually the King's Principal Secretary of State. It was owned by a succession of affluent families, including Thomas Sutton, at one stage estimated the wealthiest commoner in England, who founded Charterhouse School. It became a girls' school in the seventeenth century, and has since been home to a variety of Huguenot silk weavers, merchants, sea captains, schoolmistresses, and clergy. Although altered a good deal over the years, its front considerably modified in the Georgian period, it remains an essentially Tudor house. Fine oak panelling, original brickwork, and carved fireplaces have survived intact, together with carefully presented evidence of the changes effected in later periods. Owned by the National Trust since 1938, Sutton House reopened in 1993 after a substantial effort by local campaigners and a three-year restoration project. An exhibition tells the history of the house and its former occupants.

Tate Britain

Millbank, London SW1P 4RG

www.tate.org.uk

Open: Daily, 10:00 AM–5:50 PM (last admission, 5:00 PM); also open
6:00 PM–10:00 PM (last admission to exhibitions, 9:00 PM), first F of
each month; closed 24–26 Dec.

Admission: Free

Underground: Pimlico

Tate Britain has the finest collection of British art in the world,
its extraordinary gathering of paintings and sculpture present-
ing, in both depth and breath, that art's history from the sixteenth century to the twenty-first. The building was opened in
1897, financed by the sugar magnate, Henry Tate, and intended
to serve as the National Gallery of British Art. Almost immediately it became popularly known as the Tate Gallery, and this
title was officially confirmed in 1932. Given the additional
responsibility of forming a national collection of international
modern art, the Tate continually expanded to accommodate
the growth of its twin collections, but by about 1990 it had
become clear that the holdings had greatly outgrown both the
building and the site. Two regional galleries were created, Tate
Liverpool in 1988 and Tate St. Ives in 1993, but did not in
themselves solve the problem. A new London gallery was
clearly needed to display the international modern component
of the Tate Collection, and Tate Modern opened in 2000, thus
enabling the Millbank site to revert to its original function and
serve as the national gallery of British art.

Tate Britain's collections are shown in broadly chronological sequence and begin with the Tudor and Stuart Collection, immensely strong in portraiture and including examples by Gheeraerts, van Dyck, and Nicholas Hilliard, whose portrait of Elizabeth I is dated around 1575 (he became Queen Elizabeth I's painter after 1570, though working mainly in miniature). Two famous images here are *The Cholmondeley Ladies* and David Des Granges' *The Saltonstall Family*, with its curious mingling of the living and the dead. Sir Godfrey Kneller succeeded Sir Peter Lely as the King's painter, and they are both well represented. The eighteenth-century rooms feature the "Grand Manner," dominant in the mid-eighteenth century, notably in the hands of Sir Joshua Reynolds but also marking some works by Gainsborough and Hogarth. They also pay special attention to the giants of the Romantic age. William Blake and Samuel Palmer are explored in the context of the British twentieth-century artists influenced by them, including Graham Sutherland, Paul Nash, John Piper, Cecil Collins, and Henry Moore. John Constable is central to the extended display of British landscape and Romantic painting, which also features David Wilkie, William Etty, Benjamin Haydon, and John Martin. In the specially built Clore Gallery, the unique Turner Collection of about 300 paintings and many thousands of sketches and watercolours is housed. Opened in 1987, it reunited several parts of the Turner bequest, and spread over nearly a dozen rooms, it is a superb, unrivalled collection.

The extensive collections of Victorian paintings explore the devotion to both narrative on a small, even domestic, scale and to spectacle, large subjects on large picture spaces, as well as nineteenth-century artists' forays into the Near East and their responses to industrialism. There is a splendid range of paintings from the Pre-Raphaelite Brotherhood, iconic works by

Dante Gabriel Rossetti, Holman Hunt, and Millais, as well as those associated with them, particularly Ford Madox Brown. There are innumerable, strikingly familiar nineteenth-century images such as Waterhouse's *Lady of Shalott*, Burne-Jones's *King Cophetua and the Beggar-Maid*, Whistler's *Nocturne: Blue and Gold*, and his *Symphony in White*. The Tate is also particularly noted for its holdings of early twentieth-century British art, marvellous paintings and sculptures from the heroic age of modernism, and the enthusiast will find, as well as a fine range of pictures from the Camden School (particularly Walter Sickert), Mark Gertler's *Merry-Go-Round*, David Bomberg's *In the Hold*, C. W. R. Nevinson's *La Mitrailleuse*, and Henri Gaudier-Brzeska's sculptures, *Red Stone Dancer* and *Bird Swallowing a Fish*, in one room and in the company of other admirable pieces.

There is fine work by John Singer Sargent, Eric Gill, and Paul Nash; Stanley Spencer's *Swan Upping at Cookham* is here, and one of his remarkable resurrection pieces. Here too are Jacob Epstein, David Hockney, Walter Sickert, and Howard Hodgkin. There are fine holdings of Francis Bacon and Lucien Freud, Barbara Hepworth, and Christopher Wood. The list is, quite simply, endless, running on through Pop Art and Tachisme (with work by Patrick Heron and Gillian Ayres) to the present. And, each year, Tate Britain hosts the reliably controversial Turner Prize competition and holds an exhibition of recent work by the four shortlisted artists.

Tate Modern

Bankside, London SE1 9TG
020 7887 8000
www.tate.org.uk

Open: Su–Th, 10:00 AM–6:00 PM; F–Sa, 10:00 AM–10:00 PM
Admission: Free (except for special exhibitions)
Underground: Southwark/Blackfriars/London Bridge

Created in the year 2000 from a disused power station in the heart of London, Tate Modern displays the national collection of international modern art, defined as art since 1900. International painting pre-1900 is found at the National Gallery, and sculpture is at the Victoria & Albert Museum. Over twenty-five million people have visited Tate Modern since its opening, and it has become a true London landmark in a previously underdeveloped area as well as the most popular museum of modern art in the world.

Designed for less than two million visitors a year, the museum consistently attracts at least twice that number. A completely new building is planned, with far more space for both exhibitions and other educational and recreational features. The Tate collection of modern and contemporary art represents all the major movements from Fauvism onward. It includes important masterpieces by both Picasso and Matisse and one of the world's finest museum collections of Surrealism, including works by Dalí, Ernst, Magritte, and Miró. Its substantial holdings of Abstract Expressionism include major works by Pollock as well as the nine Seagram Murals by Rothko, which constitute the famous Tate Rothko Room. There is an in-depth collection of the Russian pioneer of abstract art Naum Gabo, and an important group of sculpture and paintings by Giacometti.

Tate has significant collections of Pop Art, including major works by Lichtenstein and Warhol; Minimal Art; and Conceptual Art; as well as particularly rich holdings of post-1980s art. The gallery has recently rehung its collections displays for the first time since the gallery opened. There are four wings located on Levels 3 and 5. At the heart of each is a large central display, or hub, which focuses on a key period in the development of twentieth-century art. These four seminal periods are Surrealism, Minimalism, postwar innovations in abstraction and figuration, and the three linked movements of Cubism, Futurism, and Vorticism. Around these hubs a diverse range of related displays present works that anticipated, challenged, or responded to these four major movements. Moving back and forwards in time, these displays reflect the ongoing dialogue between past and present and suggest contemporary perspectives for approaching and reassessing the past.

On Level 3, Poetry and Dream presents Surrealism and Beyond, the seminal figures of Duchamp, Ernst, Tanguy, Klee, Dalí, and Magritte set beside others who responded to the movement in diverse ways, these ranging from Calder and Paul Nash to Picabia, Francis Bacon, and Henry Moore. Material Gestures explores painting and sculpture from the 1940s and 1950s, showing how new forms of abstraction and expressive figuration emerged in post-war Europe and America. The exhibition in Room 2 has several fine pieces by Giacometti plus work by Pollock, Kline, Guston, and Bacon. Room 3 is given over to a series of murals by Mark Rothko. Other rooms explore related topics and groupings. On Level 5, the central space's Cubism, Futurism, and Vorticism display has some marvellous items: David Bomberg's *Ju-Jitsu* and the metal torso from Jacob Epstein's *Rock-Drill* (unsettling even without the original drill), works by Braque and Juan Gris, Wyndham Lewis, Picasso, and less widely known painters such as Jessica Dismorr.

Surrounding displays are concerned with some of the ways in which the influence of such movements manifested itself later. There are rooms devoted to movements (Pop Art), After Impressionism (Bonnard, Vuillard, Matisse, Cézanne), pairings and single figures (Richard Hamilton, Martin Parr), and technical innovations (collage, assemblage). Idea and Object concentrates on Minimalism, its antecedents, such as Constructivism and the ready-made, and later developments. Room 3 has a broader display of works by artists as varied as Donald Judd, Carl Andre, and Frank Stella; some rooms are devoted to single artists (Dan Flavin, Joseph Beuys). Level 4, sandwiched between the two thematic floors, hosts the temporary exhibitions.

Theatre Museum

The Theatre Museum (National Museum of the Performing Arts) closed in January 2007 due to difficulties in raising the necessary funds for refurbishment of the Covent Garden building. The Victoria & Albert Museum, owners of the Theatre Museum, plan to display the collections in a new gallery on their main South Kensington site. They will continue the work of documenting and recording live performances, collecting photographs, press cuttings, and programmes from more than 200 venues in the UK.

Dates and opening times for the new gallery have not yet been announced. Updates will be available on the new Web site: www.vam.ac.uk/vastatic/theatre/.

The Theatre Museum tells the story of the evolution of the performing arts from Shakespeare's age to the present. Its collections are the most extensive in the world and include costumes, designs, publicity materials, books and manuscripts, video recordings, and paintings. The aim is to enable visitors to reconstruct both performances and the lives of the performers, and the collections cover all the performing arts, from drama to dance, puppetry, circus, and music hall. There are models of performance spaces and auditoriums, costume and make-up demonstrations, and workshops. The museum's holdings run to over a million theatre programmes and playbills, the earliest dating from 1704. Video has increasingly geared collecting policy toward contemporary performance and oral history, adding a vital new dimension to the more traditional forms of documentation the museum continues to gather.

Tower Bridge Exhibition

Tower Bridge, London SE1 2UP

www.towerbridge.org.uk

Open: 10:00 AM–6:30 PM (last admission 5:30 PM), Apr–Sep; 9:30 AM–6:00 PM (last admission 5:45 PM), Oct–Mar

Admission: £6.00; Concessions, £4.50; Children under 16, £3.00; Children under 5, Free

Underground: Tower Hill

One of the most recognizable bridges in the world, Tower Bridge has stood over the River Thames in London since 1894. Originally, London Bridge was the only crossing over the Thames, and though new bridges were built as the city expanded, these were all to the west of London Bridge, since the area to the east had become a busy port. In the second half of the nineteenth century, pressure from the public, whose journeys were constantly extended by hours, became irresistible, and the Corporation of London, responsible for that section of the Thames, set the project in motion. It took eight years, over 11,000 tons of steel, and the efforts of more than 400 construction workers. The Victorian Engine Rooms, home to the original steam engines that used to power the Bridge lifts, are accessible to visitors, who can also take advantage of the specially designed windows along the walkways to take photographs unobscured by glass.

Tower of London

HM Tower of London, London EC3N 4AB
0870 7515177
www.hrp.org.uk/TowerOfLondon

Open: Tu–Sa, 9:00 AM–6:00 PM, Su–M, 10:00 AM–6:00 PM,
Mar–Oct; Tu–Sa, 9:00 AM–5:00 PM, Su–M 10:00 AM–5:00 PM,
Nov–Feb (last admission one hour before closing); closed 24–26 Dec
and 1 Jan.
Admission: £16.00; Concessions, £13.00; Children under 16, £9.50;
Children under 5, Free
Underground: Tower Hill

The Tower of London is one of the world's most famous and
spectacular fortresses, with a 900-year history as royal palace,
mint, arsenal, menagerie, jewel house, prison, and place of execution. Henry VI, among many others, was put to death here;
Elizabeth I was held prisoner, as was William Penn; much later,
Rudolf Hess was held here, and enemy spies were executed during both World Wars. There is a permanent display on the
theme of prisoners, incorporating visual and audio special effects.
Today the medieval defences remain relatively unchanged, except
at the western entrance. The Crown Jewels, first shown to the
public during Charles II's reign, include crowns (nearly a dozen
on display, including the Imperial State Crown, worn by the
Queen at the opening of Parliament), sceptres, and swords used
during state occasions and ceremonies. The oldest gem in the
Imperial Crown is Edward the Confessor's sapphire. The
Sceptre with the Cross, containing the largest cut diamond in
the world, is also present. The White Tower, the oldest surviving building here, was completed by 1100. The Armour Gallery
includes three suits made for Henry VIII.

2 Willow Road

2 Willow Road, Hampstead, London NW3 1TH
020 7435 6166
www.nationaltrust.org.uk

Open: Apr–Oct, Thu–Sa, noon–5:00 PM; Mar and Nov, Sa only,
noon–5:00 PM. Tours at noon, 1:00 PM, and 2:00 PM; self-guided,
3:00 PM–5:00 PM.
Admission: £4.90; Children, £2.50. Joint ticket with Fenton House
available.
Underground: Hampstead

The architect Ernö Goldfinger designed and built this house as
his family home in 1939. The central house of a terrace of three,
completed just before the outbreak of the Second World War,
it is one of Britain's most important examples of Modernist
architecture and is filled with furniture also designed by
Goldfinger. Goldfinger's initial plans, drawn up in 1936, were for
a block of flats with studios, with one for his own family, but
these were rejected by the London County Council. He exper-
imented with several other designs before coming up with the
final, acceptable terrace of three houses, with a large central
home, almost square in plan, for the Goldfinger family. The
double-height studio was abandoned in favour of a change in
floor level to correspond with the various functions of the
house. A flat roof, allowing staircase and bathrooms to be lit
from above, saved the walls for bedrooms and a nursery. The art
collection features significant works by Bridget Riley, Max
Ernst, Marcel Duchamp, and Henry Moore, among others.

UCL Art Collection

Strang Print Room, University College London, Gower Street, London
WC1E 6BT
020 7679 2540
www.ucl.ac.uk/silva/museums/uclart/index

Open: M–F, 1:00 PM–5:00 PM, and by appointment at other times.
The other art collections are available by appointment.
Admission: Free
Underground: Warren Street/Euston Square

The UCL Art Collections contain over 10,000 objects,
including paintings, drawings, prints, and sculpture dating from
1490 to the present day. Works on paper are housed in the
Strang Print Room, and paintings and sculpture are displayed
in public rooms around the college. The collection was founded in 1847 with a gift of the sculpture models and drawings of
the neo-classical artist John Flaxman. It has since benefited
hugely from other major bequests: the Grote bequest of 1872
included an important group of sixteenth-century German
works; the Vaughan bequest of 1900 included drawings by
Turner and De Wint, Rembrandt etchings, and early proofs
and states of Turner's *Liber Studiorum* and Constable's *English
Landscape Scenery*; and the Sherborn bequest of 1937 added
many rare and important prints to the collection, including an
early edition of Dürer's Apocalypse woodcuts and early states
and proofs from Van Dyck's *Iconographia*.

The holdings include the collection of prizewinning student
work from the Slade School of Art dating back to 1890: by
Stanley Spencer, Augustus John, Edward Wadsworth, and

Paula Rego, while other gifts and purchases have added important work by David Bomberg, Gwen John, William Orpen, Walter Sickert, Dora Carrington, and Winifred Knights.

Vestry House Museum

Vestry Road, Walthamstow, London E17 9NH

020 8509 1917

www.walthamforest.gov.uk/index/leisure/museums-galleries/vestry-house-museum.htm

Open: M–F, 10:00 AM–1:00 PM, 2:00 PM–5:30 PM; Sa, 10:00 AM–1:00 PM, 2:00 PM–5:00 PM; closed on Sundays and Bank Holidays.

Admission: Free

Underground: Walthamstow Central (Victoria Line); five-minute walk to museum

Vestry House, in the village of Church End, Walthamstow, is the Local History Museum for the London Borough of Waltham Forest and has several collections of items connected with the area dating back to the mid-nineteenth century. The Domestic Life Gallery displays utensils used for washing, ironing, cooking, and for serving food, while the Toys and Games Gallery looks at typical toys that were played with or manufactured in Waltham Forest during the nineteenth and twentieth centuries. There is a reconstruction of a typical local Victorian parlour from about 1890, and the Costume Gallery contains examples of clothing that include a Victorian wedding dress and a wedding dress from the Second World War. The main individual exhibit, permanently on display, is the Bremer Car, constructed in 1892 and one of the claimants to being the oldest British-built petrol-driven car.

Victoria and Albert Museum

Cromwell Road, London SW7 2RL

020 7942 2000

www.vam.ac.uk

Open: Daily, 10:00 AM–5:45 PM (10:00 AM–10:00 PM, F); closed 24–26 Dec.

Admission: Free

Underground: South Kensington

The V & A at South Kensington is one of the world's great museums of art and design. Founded in 1852 as the Museum of Manufactures in the wake of the Great Exhibition of the previous year, it was renamed by Queen Victoria in 1899. Spread over six levels, the museum's holdings of extraordinary objects, ceramics, furniture, costume, glass, jewellery, metalwork, photographs, sculpture, textiles, and paintings, drawn from the cultures of the world over several thousand years are vast in scope and astonishingly varied. There is a constant and ambitious programme of refurbishment and redevelopment, which means that some galleries will inevitably be inaccessible at any time (it is always worth checking the programme of gallery closures if you plan to see specific items). It also means frequent impressive additions or radically enhanced displays. One example is the 2006 opening of the Jameel Gallery of Islamic Art, a new home for several hundred items, including glassware, textiles, and ceramics, ranging from the eighth century to the early twentieth and from Spain to Afghanistan, Turkey, and Iran. It also provides a showcase for the famous Ardabil Carpet, the oldest known dated carpet. There are also constant additions to the holdings, such as the extraordinary scroll painting, 4.1

metres long by 55.9 centimetres wide (some thirteen feet by two), by Madhu Chitrakar depicting the attacks on New York on 11 September 2001. The scroll painting, as a means of conveying information about events of huge significance, is still practised in West Bengal, and Chitrakar painted this one in the village of West Medinipur in about 2004.

In addition to the Jameel Gallery, Level 1 offers the stunning Asian Galleries. The V & A holds more than 70,000 works of art from China, Japan, and Korea, ranging in time from 200 BC to the contemporary. Its important collection of Chinese artefacts includes extensive holdings of Chinese export art, brought back by Western merchants, and sculpture, together with textiles, furniture, ornaments, and porcelain. The holdings of Japanese ceramics, netsuke, prints, textiles, swords, and armour are among the finest in the Western world, while those from India and South East Asia comprise nearly 60,000 objects, including about 10,000 textiles and 6,000 paintings. The Nehru Gallery of Indian Art is very strong in the arts of the Mughal Empire but also covers the later period of British rule, which produced one of the most famous single items in the museum: "Tippoo's Tiger," a remarkable, life-sized model of a tiger devouring a British soldier, which emits shrieks when played, and has aroused great admiration for 200 years. Tipu was the Sultan of Mysore between 1782 and 1799 and was killed when the British captured his capital, Seringapatam. Tipu's extreme liking for tigers (and extreme dislike of the British) may account for the commissioned piece.

On Levels 2 and 4 are the British Galleries, concentrating on the years 1500–1900 and composing the most comprehensive collection of British design and applied art in the world. There are some remarkable items on display, among them two famous beds: the Great Bed of Ware, which dominates Room 57, is enormous, twice the size of a normal bed of the end of the sixteenth century; and the State Bed from Melville House, Fife, made in 1700 for George, 1st Earl of Melville, for the Apartment of State at his new palace, still has its original luxury hangings and is a truly spectacular object. Also here are Henry VIII's writing desk and James II's wedding suit, together with wonderful portrait miniatures of Elizabeth I. In Gallery 52b, where Taking Tea jostles Spitalfield Silks, there are beautiful designs for woven silk that are the work of Anna Maria Garthwaite, an eighteenth-century freelance textile designer, and, not far away, the astonishing embroidery from Stoke Edith House. The galleries also feature the top British designers of the times, plus the leading manufacturers, and so include work by Chippendale, Morris, Mackintosh, Wedgwood, and Liberty.

On Levels 4 and 6, the Ceramics collection is one of the cornerstones of the Victoria and Albert Museum, ranging from ancient Egyptian artefacts to contemporary studio pottery and industrially designed ceramics. The Furniture and Furnishings collection consists of more than 14,000 pieces from Britain, Europe, and America, dating from the Middle Ages to the present day, and includes such related objects as architectural and decorative woodwork, musical instruments, leatherwork, and clocks. The V & A also holds the National Collection of Glass: more than 6,000 pieces, from the Middle East, Europe, and America, which illustrate the 4,000-year history of glass.

Drawing from the unparalleled collections of the RIBA and the V&A, the new Architecture gallery explores its subject through original drawings, models, photographs, and building fragments. From Classical Rome to the twenty-first century, from East to West, and from the everyday semi to the landmark building, some 180 exhibits survey over 2,500 years of architecture. On Level 3, the Metalwork collection includes the newly displayed national collection of English silver, as well as ironwork, continental silver, arms and armour, enamels, brasswork, pewter, and medieval metalwork of international importance.

Paintings in the Victoria and Albert Museum's collection include superlative holdings of British watercolours, pastels, and portrait miniatures as well as some 2,500 British and European oil paintings. The collections were largely formed from a series of gifts from nineteenth-century collectors and offer a unique insight into Victorian picture-collecting practice. The Prints Collection, famous for encompassing both fine art and commercial production, includes Renaissance prints, topographical and portrait prints, greeting cards, and commercial graphics. It also contains the national collections of posters and of wallpapers and represents all the main printmaking processes, through its outstanding collection of printmaking tools and equipment, as well as the prints themselves, and its presentation of the book as object, with examples of rare and early books, illustration and illumination, chapbooks, comics and children's literature, calligraphy, and manuscript letters.

V & A Museum of Childhood

Cambridge Heath Road, London E2 9PA

020 8983 5200

www.museumofchildhood.org.uk

Open: Sa–Th, 10:00 AM–5:45 PM (last admission 5:30 PM); closed 24–26 Dec and 1 Jan.

Admission: Free

Underground: Bethnal Green

The Bethnal Green Museum, a branch of the Victoria and Albert Museum, opened in 1872 and was intended to serve a less privileged area of London. Its holdings represent one of the oldest and most extensive collections of children's toys and games in existence, covering 400 years. The emphasis on childhood emerged in the 1920s; it was officially reclassified in 1974. There are fine displays of dolls (ceramic, wooden, and rag), children's clothing, construction and learning toys, and a remarkable collection of dollhouses, ranging from the Nuremberg House, dating from 1673, to a late eighteenth-century dollhouse named after the writer Denton Welch, who restored it in the 1930s. There are also illuminating features on children's authors and early childbirth practices and galleries displaying the social history of childhood, with some fascinating photographs. The exhibits include a particularly fine collection of toy theatres; mechanical and clockwork toys, particularly German; and examples of games and puzzles from different parts of the British Empire.

Wallace Collection

Hertford House, Manchester Square, London W1U 3BN

020 7563 9500

www.wallacecollection.org/

Open: Daily, 10:00 AM–5:00 PM; closed 24–26 Dec.

Admission: Free

Underground: Bond Street/Baker Street

This remarkable and nationally important collection was assembled by one family over several generations. Paintings, drawings, sculptures, porcelain, armour, and much else was accumulated by several members of the Seymour-Conway family, particularly Richard, the 4th Marquess of Hertford, who devoted the last thirty years of his life to collecting on a grand scale. Many of the nineteenth-century French and English paintings, the Oriental arms and armour, and the bulk of the extensive holdings of Dutch art were acquired during that period. In 1870, the marquess's son, Sir Richard Wallace, purchased Hertford House, and when his widow died in 1897, she bequeathed the house and its contents to the nation, with the condition that the collection remain as it was. It opened to the public three years later. There are nearly 800 paintings in the collection, ranging across five centuries, but its fame is based on its holdings of eighteenth-century French art.

Watteau and Boucher are well represented, and the paintings by Fragonard include his famous *The Swing*. There are works by Claude, Decamps, and Horace Vernet, and Poussin's celebrated *A Dance to the Music of Time*. The splendid range of Dutch and Flemish work offers Rembrandt's portrait of his son Titus;

five paintings each by Hobbema, Gabriel Metsu, and Jan Steen; four by Jacob van Ruisdael; and half a dozen by Philip Wouwermans. One very popular feature is the Franz Hals picture, *The Laughing Cavalier*. There are also works by Cuyp, Gerard ter Borch, and Brouwer. There are notable portraits by Gainsborough, Reynolds, and Romney—all of whom produced a portrait of Mrs. Mary Robinson as "Perdita"—and several fine Canaletto views of Venice, as well as other notable treatments of the same city by Francesco Guardi.

The Velazquez portrait *Lady with a Fan* is here, as are four watercolours by Turner, Titian's *Perseus and Andromeda*, a fascinating gathering of Richard Parkes Bonington's oils and watercolours, and a group of Murillos. Apart from oils, watercolours, and drawings, there are sculptures by Houdon and Roubiliac, bronze statuettes, and miniatures. Outstanding even among the Wallace Collection's many other treasures is the extraordinary collection of porcelain, with fine examples of English slipware, Meissen, and Chinese but specifically including what is widely regarded as the best collection of Sèvres held in a museum. Mention must also be made of the French furniture and Venetian glass, mainly from the sixteenth and seventeenth centuries, and a collection of international significance, second in Britain only to the Royal Armouries, of European and Oriental armour, shown in four galleries on the upper floor.

Wandsworth Museum

The Courthouse, 1 Garratt Lane, London SW18 4AQ
020 8871 7074
www.wandsworth.gov.uk/Home/LeisureandTourism/Museum
Open: Tu–F, 10:00 AM–5:00 PM; Sa–Su, 2:00 PM–5:00 PM
Admission: Free
Underground: East Putney (fifteen-minute walk)
Train: Wandsworth (ten-minute walk)
Bus: 28, 37, 39, 44, 87, 156, 170, 220, 270, 337, 485

The museum is devoted to the history of Wandsworth and the transformation of the area over thousands of years. A permanent display, The Story of Wandsworth, tells the story of the area covered by the present borough from prehistoric times to the present day. There are interactive exhibits and other displays that include reconstructions of a Victorian parlour and the interior of a chemist's shop, and a model of central Wandsworth in 1865 showing the town, the three great mills on the River Wandle, and the celebrated local brewery.

Wellcome Institute

183 Euston Road, London NW1 2BE
020 7679 8100
www.wellcome.ac.uk/node6500.html

Underground: Euston/Euston Square

Currently undergoing a major transformation, the Wellcome Collection will open in the summer of 2007. It will provide a home for the renowned Wellcome Medical Library—more than a million items, including books, prints, drawings, manuscripts, moving images, and sound recordings. A new ground-floor gallery will play host to a programme of temporary exhibitions, building on the success of recent Wellcome Trust shows at the Science Museum, such as Pain and Future Face. Upstairs, there will be a permanent installation of the Medicine Man exhibition, originally held at the British Museum in 2003 when it attracted over 200,000 visitors. Another permanent gallery will explore modern medicine through a mixture of science and art exhibits.

Wellington Arch

Apsley Way, Hyde Park Corner, London W1J 7JZ

020 7930 2726

www.english-heritage.org.uk

Open: W–Su and Bank Holidays, 10:00 AM–5:00 PM, Apr–Oct; W–Su, 10:00 AM–4:00 PM, Nov–Mar; closed 24–26 Dec, 1 Jan.

Admission: £3.20; Concessions, £2.40; Children, £1.60. Joint tickets available with Apsley House.

Underground: Hyde Park Corner

The Wellington Arch has undergone dramatic changes in both composition and location. When first erected in 1828, it was topped by a huge statue of the Duke of Wellington on horseback, which was widely ridiculed. When the road was widened in 1882, the arch was moved to its present location at Hyde Park Corner. The Decimus Burton statue was replaced by Adrian Jones' substantial bronze *Peace Descending on the Quadriga of War*. Visitors can take the lift to viewing platforms just below the sculpture and enjoy superb views of the Royal Parks and the Houses of Parliament. There are exhibitions recounting the history of the arch, which includes a spell as the smallest police station in London. The Arch is opposite Apsley House, the London home of the Duke of Wellington (see separate entry).

Wesley's House and Museum of Methodism

49 City Road, Islington, London EC1Y 1AU
020 7253 2262
www.wesleyschapel.org.uk

Open: M–Sa, 10:00 AM–4:00 PM; Su, noon–1:45 PM; closed every
Thursday between 12:45 PM and 1:30 PM (for service), between
Christmas and New Year, and on public and Bank Holidays, except
Good Friday.
Admission: Free
Underground: Old Street

Built by John Wesley in 1779, this Georgian town house was
his home for the last eleven winters of his life, when not touring and preaching to Methodist societies around the country.
The house contains a great deal of Wesleyan memorabilia, and
several rooms of great interest are accessible, including his
prayer room, bedroom, and study. The neighbouring chapel,
described by Wesley as "perfectly neat but not fine," was
designed by George Dance the Younger, surveyor to the City
of London, and built in 1778. It houses a small museum that
provides an excellent introduction to the story of Methodism
from its founding to the present day. It contains one of the
world's largest collections of Wesleyan ceramics, a number of
paintings, and other objects of significance in the development
of Methodism both at home and abroad. Wesley is buried
behind the chapel; across the road from the house is the famous
nonconformist cemetery, Bunhill (derived from "Bone Hill")
Fields, where William Blake, John Bunyan, Daniel Defoe, and
George Fox, the founder of Quakerism, are buried.

Westminster Abbey Chapter House and Museum

Chapter House, East Cloisters, Westminster Abbey, London SW1P 3PE
020 7222 5152
www.westminster-abbey.org

Open: Daily, 10:30 AM–4:00 PM (may close for special events)
Admission: Free
Underground: St. James's Park/Westminster

The museum is housed in the undercroft beneath the former monks' dormitory, an area of the abbey that dates back almost to the foundation of the Norman church by Edward the Confessor in 1065. The centrepiece of the exhibition is the abbey's collection of funeral effigies, made for every monarch from the time of Henry V until around 1700 and carried on top of their coffins during their final journey. But famous commoners who could afford the expense also had them made, including Frances, Duchess of Richmond, a favourite of Charles II, chosen by him as the model for Britannia, an image which is still the seal of the Bank of England and appears on every one of the notes it issues on behalf of the Royal Mint. In the East Cloister is the octagonal Chapter House, one of the largest in England, where the monks met every day for prayers dating from the 1250s. The House of Commons regularly used the room in the fourteenth century, before they transferred to the Palace of Westminster. Restored in Victorian times by Sir Gilbert Scott, the room is lavishly adorned with sculpture and wall paintings of the Apocalypse. It contains one of the finest medieval tile pavements in England, while the windows incorporate both Victorian stained glass and new postwar designs.

William Morris Gallery

Lloyd Park, Forest Road, Walthamstow, London E17 4PP

020 8527 3782

www.lbwf.gov.uk/wmg

Open: Tu–Sa, 10:00 AM–1:00 PM, 2:00 PM–5:00 PM; first Su of each month, 10:00 AM–1:00 PM, 2:00 PM–5:00 PM; closed 24–26 Dec and public holidays.

Admission: Free

Underground: Walthamstow Central

The William Morris Gallery occupies what was the Morris family home from 1848 to 1856 and was opened by Prime Minister Clement Attlee in 1950. There are permanent displays of fabrics, rugs, carpets, wallpapers, furniture, stained glass, and painted tiles designed by Morris himself as well as by Burne-Jones, Dante Gabriel Rossetti, Ford Madox Brown, and others associated with the firm of Morris, Marshall, Faulkner & Company. Outstanding exhibits include Morris's medieval-style helmet and sword, made as props for the Pre-Raphaelite murals at the Oxford Union; the original design for Trellis (the earliest of Morris's many wallpapers); the Woodpecker tapestry woven at Morris's Merton Abbey workshops; and the Kelmscott Press edition of Chaucer. There are also displays of furniture, textiles, ceramics, and glass by Morris's followers in the Arts and Crafts movement, including William De Morgan, May Morris, C. F. A. Voysey, and Selwyn Image. The collections of applied art are complemented by the Brangwyn Gift of paintings, drawings, and prints by the Pre-Raphaelites and other Victorian and later artists, as well as works by Frank Brangwyn himself.

Wimbledon Lawn Tennis Museum

The All England Lawn Tennis Club, Church Road Wimbledon, London
SW19 5AE
020 8946 6131
www.wimbledon.org

🍽️

Open: Daily, 10:30 AM–5:00 PM Closed, middle Sunday of
Championships and Monday immediately following, 24–26 Dec, 1 Jan.
Admission: £8.50; Concessions, £7.50; Children, £4.75 (combined
tickets to include guided tour of club also available)
Underground: Southfields/South Wimbledon (then bus 493)

Established in 1977 as a part of the centenary celebrations of
the founding of the All England Lawn Tennis Association, the
museum is designed to tell the story of the sport's development, from its beginnings in ancient Greece to the present day.
The new museum opened in the spring of 2006 with greatly
enhanced audiovisual resources and interactive displays, particularly those concerned with the science of tennis and the effects
of international competition upon the players' bodies and their
equipment. There is an extensive display of tennis fashions,
from 1880s outfits through the original Lacoste jacket of the
1920s to the outfits donated most recently by Roger Federer,
Amélie Mauresmo, and Andre Agassi. An interactive exhibit
allows the visitor to feel the weight difference between male
and female clothing worn in 1884. A display of rackets is
enhanced by touch screen information and TV footage, detailing each racket's technology and story; and the Championship
trophies for both Men's and Women's Singles, dating respec-
tively from 1887 and 1886, are on display.

Wimbledon Society Museum of Local History

22 Ridgway, Wimbledon, London SW19 4QN

0208 296 9914

www.wimbledonmuseum.org.uk

Open: Sa–Sun, 2:30 PM–5:00 PM; other times by arrangement

Admission: Free

Underground: Wimbledon

Train: Wimbledon Station

Bus: 93 and 200

The museum ranges over 3,000 years of Wimbledon history; in fact, some of the tools and flint arrowheads used by those who lived and hunted on Wimbledon Common have been dated to 100,000 BC. Other exhibits illustrate the dramatic changes in the extent and nature of Wimbledon brought about by the coming of the railway in 1838, and there are mementoes and illustrations from the huge rifle-shooting contest, the largest in the country, that used to take place on the Common. Thousands of spectators attended, and a horse-drawn tramway transported people from one part of the site to another. In 1798, the Prime Minister, William Pitt (the Younger), fought a duel on the Common with George Tierney, later leader of the opposition Whig party and Master of the Mint, whom he had accused of want of patriotism.

Wimbledon Windmill Museum

Windmill Road, Wimbledon Common, London SW19 5NR

020 8947 2825

www.wimbledonwindmillmuseum.org.uk

Open: Sa, 2:00 PM–5:00 PM, Su and Bank Holidays, 11:00 AM–5:00 PM, Apr–Oct; Nov–Mar, groups only, by appointment

Admission: £1.00; Children, 50p

Underground: Wimbledon (then bus 93)

On the northern edge of Wimbledon Common, the old village windmill was built by a local carpenter, William March, in 1817. It was converted into cottages in the 1860s, and Lord Baden-Powell, founder of the scouts association, lived in the mill house while he was writing *Scouting for Boys*. The mill has been subject to several restorations, and in the late 1990s, the sails were brought back to working order. The museum contains numerous working models of windmills that tell the story of their development in several countries from the original Persian and Greek models. In the entrance is a display showing how the mill itself was constructed, and there are many examples of milling equipment on the upper floor. Children are encouraged to try grinding wheat, lifting heavy sacks with the help of a block and tackle, and using a pestle and mortar or a hand quern, supported by push button–operated commentaries.

Further Afield

Barnet Museum

31 Wood Street, Barnet, Herts EN5 4BE
020 8440 8066
www.barnetmuseum.co.uk/
Open: Tu–Th, 2:30 PM–4:30 PM; Sa, 10:30 AM–12:30 PM, 2:00 PM–4:00 PM; closed Sundays, Mondays, and Fridays.
Admission: Free, but donations always welcome.
Train: High Barnet
Bus: 107, 184, 263, 307; stop outside or opposite museum.

Collections reflect the development of Chipping Barnet and the surrounding area.

Bethlem Royal Hospital Archives and Museum

Monks Orchard Road, Beckenham, Kent BR3 2BX
020 8776 4307
www.bethlemheritage.org.uk
Open: M–F, 9:30 AM–5:00 PM, but telephone first.
Admission: Free
Train: Eden Park (from Charing Cross, Waterloo East, or London Bridge)

The museum includes historical collections of unique interest and importance in the field of mental health.

Danson House

Danson Park, Bexleyheath DA6 8HL
020 8303 6699
www.dansonhouse.com
Open: Easter–Oct, W, Thu, Su, and Bank Holidays, 11:00 AM–5:00 PM

Admission: £5.00; Concessions, £4.50; Children (accompanied), Free
Train: Bexleyheath (from London Bridge or Charing Cross)

Designed by Sir Robert Taylor, architect of the Bank of England, this is arguably one of the finest examples of English Palladian architecture in the south east of England.

Down House

Bromley, Kent BR6 7JT
01689 859119
www.english-heritage.org.uk/server/show/conProperty.102
Open: W–Su, Bank Holidays, 11:00 AM–5:00 PM (Apr–Jun); Daily, 11:00 AM–5:00 PM (Jul–Aug); W–Su, 11:00 AM–4:00 PM (Nov–mid Dec); closed, 17 Dec–29 Feb; W–Su, 11:00 AM–4:00 PM (1 Mar–20 Mar). Advisable to phone first, due to current programme of building work.
Admission: £6.90; Concessions, £5.20; Children, £3.50
Train: Orpington, then R8 bus.

Built in the early eighteenth century, this was the home of Charles Darwin from 1842, where he worked on *The Origin of Species* and other major projects.

Forty Hall

Forty Hill, Enfield, Middlesex EN2 9HA
020 8363 8196
www.enfield.gov.uk/fortyhall
Open: W–Su, 11:00 AM–4:00 PM
Admission: Free
Train: Turkey Street (from Liverpool Street), and twenty-minute walk
Bus: 191 or W10 to Forty Hill roundabout

This includes the social history of the boroughs of Edmonton, Southgate, and Enfield.

Ham House

Ham, Richmond TW10 7RS
020 8940 1950
www.nationaltrust.org.uk/places/hamhouse
Open: Apr–Oct, M–W, Sa–Su, 1:00 PM–5:00 PM
Admission: £9.00, Children, £5.00
Bus: 67, 371 from Richmond or Kingston

Here is an outstanding seventeenth-century house with gardens, famous for its interiors and collections of furniture, textiles, and paintings.

Hampton Court Palace

East Molesey, Surrey KT8 9AU
0870 752 7777
www.hrp.org.uk
Open: M–Su, 10:00 AM–6:00 PM, Apr–Oct; 10:00 AM–4:30 PM, Nov–Mar
Admission: Palace, gardens, and maze, £13.00; Concessions, £10.50; Children 5–16, £6.50
Train: Waterloo to Hampton Court

The great house relinquished by Thomas Wolsey, Archbishop of York, to Henry VIII was rebuilt and extended by Henry and then by William and Mary and is home to much of the huge Royal Collection of paintings, furniture, and tapestries. Superb riverside gardens contain the famous maze.

Kew Bridge Steam Museum

Green Dragon Lane, Brentford TW8 0EN
020 8568 4757
www.kbsm.org
Open: Tu–Su, 11:00 AM–5:00 PM; closed M except Bank Holidays.

Check for when engines are in action.

Admission: £8.00 (weekends), £5.00 (weekdays), Concessions, £1.00 less; Children under 15 accompanied by adult, Free

Train: Kew Bridge (from Waterloo)

Built in the nineteenth century to supply London with water, the museum is recognised as the most important historic site of the water supply industry in Britain.

Kew Palace and Royal Botanic Gardens

Royal Botanic Gardens, Kew, Surrey TW9 3AB

Information centre and 24-hour information: 020 8332 5655

www.hrp.org.uk/KewPalace/

Kew Palace opens late Mar–Oct, 10:00 AM–5:00 PM

www.rbgkew.org.uk/visitor/visitkew.html

The Gardens open at 9:30 AM and closing times vary: early Apr to early Sep, 6:30 PM, M–F and 7:30 PM, Sa, Su and Bank Holidays; early Sep–late Oct, 6:00 PM; late Oct–early Feb, 4:15 PM. Please check for exact details.

Underground: Kew Gardens

Admission to Royal Botanic Gardens: £12.25, Concessions £10.25, Children under 17, Free

Admission to Kew Palace (entrance only with ticket to the gardens): £5, Concessions £4, children 5-16 accompanied by adult £2.50, children under 5, Free

Kew Palace, George III's family home, set in the grounds of the beautiful Royal Botanic Gardens Kew is open to visitors from late March to late October. Queen Charlotte's Cottage, the royal family's picnic retreat in the woods, is also situated within Kew Gardens. The Orangery, designed by Sir William Chambers, 1761, was once the largest glasshouse in England. See also: *Museum No 1, Marianne North Gallery*, below.

Kingston Museum

Wheatfield Way, Kingston upon Thames KT1 2PS
020 8546 5386
www.kingston.gov.uk/museum
Open: 10:00 AM–1:00 PM and 2:00 PM–5:00 PM except Wednesday,
Saturday and Sunday
Admission: Free
Train: Kingston (from Waterloo)

This museum tells the story of the borough since Saxon times.
Eadweard Muybridge, who was born here, bequeathed his
equipment and prints to the museum.

Little Holland House

40 Beeches Avenue, Carshalton SM5 3LW
020 8770 4781
www.sutton.gov.uk/leisure/heritage/lhh
Open: 1:30 PM–5:30 PM on the first Su of each month plus bank
Holiday Sundays and Mondays (except Christmas and New Year)
Admission: Free.
Train: Carshalton Beeches

The house was designed by artist and craftsman Frank
Dickinson (1874–1961) between 1902 and 1904, who drew on an
eclectic mix of Arts and Crafts and other styles.

London Motorcycle Museum

Ravenor Farm, Oldfield Lane South, Greenford, Middlesex UB6 9LD
020 8575 6644
www.motorcycle-uk.com
Open: Sa, Su, Bank Holidays, 10:00 AM–4:30 PM
Admission: £3.00; Senior Citizens, £1.50; Children 5–14, 50p;

Children under 5, Free

This is the only motorcycle museum in London, with some 80 machines on display.

Marble Hill House

Richmond Road, Twickenham TW1 2NL
020 8892 5115
www.english-heritage.org.uk/visits
Open: Apr–Oct, Sa, 10:00 AM–2:00 PM; Su and Bank Holidays, 10:00 AM–5:00 PM; Nov–Mar by appointment; closed, 24 Dec–29 Feb.
Admission: £4.20; Concessions, £3.20; Children, £2.10
Train: St. Margaret's (from Waterloo)

Marble Hill is the last complete survivor of the elegant eighteenth-century villas and gardens that bordered the Thames between Richmond and Hampton Court.

Marianne North Gallery

Kew, Richmond, Surrey TW9 3AB
020 8332 5655
www.kew.org/places/kew/mariannenorth.html
Daily from 9.30 AM: closing times vary according to season (approximately 4:00 PM in winter, 6:00 PM in summer)
Underground: Kew Gardens
Admission charge included in entrance fee to Kew Gardens

Over 800 of North's paintings of plants.

Museum Number One

Kew, Richmond, Surrey TW9 3AB
020 8332 5655
www.kew.org/places/kew/museumno1.html

Daily from 9:30 AM; closing times vary according to season (approximately 4:00 PM in winter, 6:00 PM in summer)

Underground: Kew Gardens

Admission charge included in entrance fee to Kew Gardens

Plants + People: collections displayed in a dozen of the original mahogany cabinets.

Museum of Domestic Design and Architecture

Middlesex University (Cat Hill Campus), Cat Hill, Barnet, London EN4 8HT

020 8411 5244

www.moda.mdx.ac.uk

Open: Tu–Sa, 10:00 AM–5:00 PM; Su, 2:00 PM–5:00 PM; closed Mondays, Christmas to New Year period, and Easter.

Admission: Free

Underground: Cockfosters

This museum includes a number of separate collections that build up a vivid picture of the design of domestic life in the early twentieth century.

Osterley Park

Jersey Road, Isleworth, Middlesex TW7 4RB

www.osterleypark.org.uk

Open: Mid-Mar–end Oct, W–Su and Bank Holidays, 1:00 PM–4:30 PM; Mar, Sa–Su, 1:00 PM–4:30 PM

Admission: £7.50; Children 5–16, £3.50; Children under 5, Free

Underground: Osterley

Osterley Park is a Robert Adam house set in acres of beautiful parkland and farmland.

Red House

Red House Lane, Bexleyheath DA6 8JF

01494 755588

www.nationaltrust.org.uk/main/w-vh/w-visits/w-findaplace/w-red-house.htm

Open: Mar–Dec, W–Su and Bank Holidays, 11:00 AM–4:15 PM (last admission 45 minutes before closing); closed 23 Dec–mid-Feb, M–Tu (except Bank Holidays). Guided tours only; telephone to book.

Admission: £6.40; Concessions, £3.20

Here is the home of William Morris, the only house that Morris commissioned and created.

Syon Park

Brentford, Middlesex TW8 8JF

020 8560 0882

www.syonpark.co.uk

Open: End Mar–end Oct, W, Th, Su, and Bank Holidays, 11:00 AM–5:00 PM

Admission: House and gardens, £8.00; Concessions, £7.00; Children, £4.00

Train: Kew Bridge (from Waterloo), then bus 237 or 267

This is the London home of the Duke of Northumberland, whose family have lived here for over 400 years.

Twickenham Museum

25 The Embankment, Twickenham, Middlesex TW1 3DU

020 8408 0070

www.twickenham-museum.org.uk

Open: Tu, Sa, 11:00 AM–3:00 PM; Su, 2:00 PM–4:00 PM

Admission: Free, but donations welcome.

The museum encompasses the history centre for the Thames villages of Twickenham, Whitton, Teddington, and the Hamptons.

Appendix

The following lists are thematic guides to the collections of the museums in London. All lists are in alphabetical order.

Essential Museums

British Library

British Museum

Courtauld Institute

Freud Museum

Imperial War Museum

Museum of London

National Gallery

Natural History Museum

Science Museum

Sir John Soane's

Tate Britain

Tate Modern

Victoria & Albert Museum

Wallace Collection

Artists and Writers Museums

Benjamin Franklin House

Carlyle's House

Charles Dickens Museum

Dalí Universe

Dr. Johnson's House

Handel House Museum

Hogarth's House

Keats House

Leighton House Museum

Linley Sambourne House

William Morris Gallery

2 Willow Road

ART MUSEUMS

Courtauld Institute

De Morgan Centre

Dulwich Picture Gallery

Estorick Collection of Modern Italian Art

Fleming Collection

National Gallery

National Portrait Gallery

Percival David Foundation

Queen's Gallery

Tate Britain

Tate Modern

UCL Art Collections

Victoria and Albert Museum

Wallace Collection

William Morris Gallery

MEDICAL MUSEUMS

Alexander Fleming Laboratory Museum

Anaesthesia Museum

British Optical Association

Chelsea Physic Garden

Florence Nightingale

Hunterian Museum

Old Operating Theatre Museum and Herb Garret

Royal College of Physicians

Royal Hospital Chelsea Museum

Royal London Hospital Museum

Saint Bartholomew's Hospital Museum

MUSEUMS WITH EXHIBITS FOR CHILDREN

British Museum

Brunel Engine House

Cutty Sark Clipper Ship

Golden Living Hinde History Museum

Museum of London

National Gallery

National Maritime Museum

Natural History Museum

Science Museum

V&A Museum of Childhood

Wimbledon Windmill Museum

MUSEUMS OF SCIENCE & TECHNOLOGY

British Museum

Brunel Engine House

Clockmakers Museum

Faraday Museum

Grant Museum of Zoology

Natural History Museum

Royal Observatory Greenwich

Science Museum

MILITARY HISTORY MUSEUMS

Cabinet War Rooms

Fire Power

Golden Hinde

Guards Museum

HMS Belfast

Imperial War Museum

Jewish Military Museum

Royal Air Force Museum

Royal Fusiliers Museum

Royal Hospital Chelsea

HISTORIC HOUSE MUSEUMS

Apsley House

Chiswick House

Dennis Severs' House

Fenton House

Hogarth's House

Kenwood House

Leighton House Museum

Linley Samborne House

Southside House

Spencer House

Sutton House

Index of Alternative Museum Names